Mathematics and Statistics Hacks for MySQL

Jeremy Lane

ii

Cover Photo: Dustin Shuler - Spindle - 3 - Cermak Plaza, Chicago, Illinois
Flickr flickr.com/photos/lifeontheedge/726216255

Chapter 1

Introduction

The goal of this text is to demonstrate to readers how to use MySQL software to perform computations that are common in undergraduate mathematics courses. Since this text assumes the reader has little to no experience with MySQL, the stored procedures are essentially simple to write and follow. This is done on purpose so readers may become accustomed to how MySQL operates. There is a multitude of sites dedicated to MySQL and I encourage readers to examine these sites for additional information.

The reason why MySQL is chosen as the technological companion here is quite simple, people outside of academics use it, and use it a lot. While there are a plethora of software packages available for mathematical analysis, such as *Mathematica*, *Maple*, SAS, SPSS and R, these tend to be used for very specialized fields and are not as common in everyday corporate activities. Many students who graduate high school or college will most likely be employed at a business where they will be working with databases. Either they will be entering information into a database, extracting information from the result of some algorithm applied to information in a database or actually manipulating databases to get information into a certain format. In many cases, graduates will be working with databases in some way. I thought, "If this is true, then why do we not use such tools when we teach students?" This is what inspired me to write this text.

The text itself is not a rigorous treatment of mathematics, nor is it a text to show really cool, advanced techniques with MySQL. The purpose of the text is simple: introduce stored procedures applied to mathematics. Essentially, by the end of this text, a reader could be comfortable enough with MySQL to have a foundation for working toward more advanced algorithms. The stored procedures in this text may contain commands that you are not familiar with, and that is okay. You have an abundance of tools at your disposal to understand commands: the Internet, texts on MySQL or SQL and coworkers if available. Also since MySQL and SQL are similar, many of the procedures could translate over to SQL with modifications to the syntax. It also looks good on a resume that you would have experience with MySQL or SQL if a potential career uses either of these tools in day-to-day operations.

So the audience is not career mathematicians, statisticians or data miners. It is mainly for individuals who may be pursuing other types of careers where database use is common. Those taking (or teaching) courses where mathematical procedures abound may wish to gain knowledge and understanding of this language. Experience with a software language is one benefit people have after their academics are completed. Using a language that is common in corporate operations is a major benefit when seeking employment.

I would like to thank you, the reader, for reading this text, as well as my family who supported me in this endeavor. I would also like to thank the thousands of individuals who asked questions on blog pages on the Internet and those who answered them. That has proven to me to be a valuable source of information. I hope this text will be an asset to help you build a foundation to further your adventures in MySQL. Enjoy!

Legal Matters

While it is often assumed by readers and implied by authors of codes, I state the following:

I make no warranties, express or implied, that the programs contained in this text have no errors. I cannot guarantee they meet standards of merchantability or will even suit your needs. The programs in this text should not be used for solving a problem whose incorrect solution could result in any type of injury to a person or loss of property. The author and publisher are absolved of all liability for damages, directly or indirectly resulting from your use of the programs.

Chapter 2

Syntax

Since this text focuses on stored procedures with MySQL, it is important that we understand the syntax and structure of a stored procedure. Many online sources are available for basic structure and I will repeat it here so you may have a quick reference to the basic syntax of this powerful tool in MySQL. The skeleton of a stored procedure appears as follows.

```
Delimiter \\
create procedure PROCEDURE_NAME(
in input 1 data type,
in input 2 data type,
...
out output 1 data type,
out output 2 data type,
...
)
Begin
set local variables;
loops, conditions, and other commands for the procedure;
end\\
Delimiter ;
```

There are two ways to have stored procedures and both of these ways are done in this text initially. You may have a list of inputs and outputs in the arguments of the stored procedure or you may not. When you have a stored procedure in our Query Tab with MySQL we need to call it. This is accomplished with a **call** command. You may call stored procedures as follows

call *stored procedure name(input 1, input 2, ..., output 1, output 2, ...)*

Use this statement if you have output included in your list of parameters. If you do not have output listed, you may have the following call command.

call *stored procedure name(input 1, input 2, ...)*

This command only calls the procedure to run. It will not return any values, but all values the stored procedure creates, including tables, will be accessible. To access these values use a **select** command. It is probably best to demonstrate this with a specific example. A simple stored procedure with calls to the output is given below.

```
Delimiter \\
create procedure ProcedureDemo(
in a float,
in b float,
out c float)
Begin
set @i = 1;
set @n = 10;
while @i <= @n do
set c = @i * a + b;
set @i = @i + 1;
end while;
end \\
Delimiter ;
call ProcedureDemo(1,5,@c);
select @i as counter, @n as Stopper, @c as result;
```

The output of this stored procedure is given below.

counter	Stopper	result
11	10	15

The **Delimiter** command at the beginning of the program lets MySQL know what symbol is going to be used to end the stored procedure. The Delimiter command at the end of the procedure lets MySQL know the following commands are not a part of the procedure. Many symbols can be used, but dollar signs and slashes are the most common and I will always use the backslash. This particular stored procedure has output variables in the parameter list. If we choose to not have this, our code is altered as below.

```
Delimiter \\
create procedure ProcedureDemo2(
in a float,
in b float)
Begin
set @i = 1;
set @n = 10;
while @i <= @n do
set @c = @i * a + b;
set @i = @i + 1;
```

```
end while;
end \\
Delimiter ;
call ProcedureDemo2(1,5);
select @i as counter, @n as Stopper, @c as result;
```

The output is the same, but notice the difference in the stored procedure and how the procedure is called. What if we wish to have all the values output from this procedure? We need to alter this procedure to create a table of values and then output the table rather than the last stored values in the variables. Rather than rewrite or copy the code again in a new query tab, we may simply drop the procedure *and* any associated tables. This saves time and memory since there is no need to keep a bad stored procedure in a database. So let's go back to our query and add in the following line,

```
drop procedure ProcedureDemo;
```

This will remove the procedure from the database. Now you can make the changes you wish to make and then execute the stored procedure again. Be sure to only highlight the procedure rather than execute the entire worksheet. MySQL will execute highlighted portions of queries unless you hit the lightning bolt button without any highlights. Be careful though when moving you mouse around the screen, you may inadvertently highlight code parts and have error messages return.

If we wish to add a table to our procedure to see each output, I would recommend a temporary table rather than a permanent one. Temporary tables are useful when you wish to only have a table of values available for procedures and functions rather than a permanent table. If you do not need a table except when runnig a stored procedure, go ahead and use a temporary table. If you make a mistake and need to drop the procedure, make sure you also drop the temporary table via the command,

```
drop temporary table Table_Name;
```

Now let's alter our first procedure to include all the values generated.

```
Delimiter \\
create procedure ProcedureDemo(
in a float,
in b float,
out c float)
Begin
set @i = 1;
set @n = 10;
create temporary table DemoTable( j int, value1 float, value2 float,
        result float);
while @i <= @n do
```

```
set c = @i * a + b;
insert into DemoTable(j, value1, value2, result)
values (@i, a, b, c);
set @i = @i + 1;
end while;
end \\
Delimiter ;
call ProcedureDemo(1,5,@c);
select * from DemoTable;
```

The output from this stored procedure appears below.

j	value1	value2	result
1	1	5	6
2	1	5	7
3	1	5	8
4	1	5	9
5	1	5	10
6	1	5	11
7	1	5	12
8	1	5	13
9	1	5	14
10	1	5	15

Part of programming in any language is developing your style, your perspective as to how you think it will be best to achieve solutions of problems and, arguably equally important, the presentation of such solutions. Do not be too quick to lock yourself into a specific style though as not all problems can be solved using a pre-determined method. Increasing your knowledge of commands, syntax and methods for solving problems all play a role when developing your style. The best programmers have all these skills in a dynamic-adaptable fashion rather than a static one. They often change their style to adapt to the situation rather than try to change the situation to match their style. While you examine this text, you'll notice a similar style for many of the schemes here. If you can, adjust the procedures to suit your style as you become more acquainted wth the language itself. Good luck and enjoy learning this valuable tool and increasing your abilities.

Chapter 3

Introductory Algebra

We begin our journey into mathematics using stored procedures with topics in introductory algebra. This topic offers a rich multitude of examples to start. These examples are suitable for beginners as far as complexity is concerned. It also provides opportunities to us to consider comments and error checking, which are important aspects of programming no matter the language used. There are only a few topics that are almost exclusive to an introductory algebra course.

1. Solving Some Equations

2. Factoring

3.1 Solving Some Equations

Let's begin with the solving of the linear equation: $ax + b = c$. The solution of this equation is $x = \dfrac{b - c}{a}$. If we consider an example $7x + 2 = 10$, a query would appear as follows.

```
set @a = 7.0;
set @b = 2.0;
set @c = 10.0;
select (@c - @b)/@a;
```

In order to use this, we would have to edit this query each and every time we wish to use it. A stored procedure would only require us to change the coefficients. A carefully coded stored procedure would also inform us of errors or other issues that may result from certain coefficients. Below I offer such a stored procedure.

```
Delimiter \\
create procedure linearsolver(
in a float,
in b float,
```

```
in c float,
out Answer varchar(30))
/*Program solves equation ax + b = c */
Begin
If a <> 0.0 then
select (c - b)/a as Answer;
end if;
If (a = 0 and b <> c) then
select 'No Solution' as Answer;
end if;
If (a = 0 and b = c) then
select 'Infinitely Many Solutions' as Answer;
end if;
end \\
Delimiter ;
```

As this example shows, stored procedures are much more useful to use than queries when similar calculations are to be done repeatedly. Take some time to decipher and dissect this procedure so you gain familiarity with the syntax, such as the meaning of <>. Other solving formulas may also be programmed. Below I offer a stored procedure for quadratic equations, i.e. the quadratic formula.

```
Delimiter \\
create procedure QuadraticFormula(
in a float,
in b float,
in c float,
out Real_Part_SOLN float,
out Radical_Part_SOLN char(25))
Begin
select -1.0*b/(2.0*a) into Real_Part_SOLN;
set @DIS := 0.0;
set @DIS := (select b*b - 4.0*a*c);
if @DIS < 0 then
set @DIS := round(sqrt(abs(@DIS))/(2.0*a),6);
select concat(@DIS, ' I') Into Radical_Part_SOLN;
else
select cast(round(sqrt(@DIS)/(2.0*a),6) as char) into
       Radical_Part_SOLN;
end if;
end\\
Delimiter ;
```

This procedure has two commands, the **cast** and the **concat** commands. The cast command is used to change the variable type. It is used here to "cast" the result of the square root computation into a character string. This enables the imaginary unit, i, to be added to the string of characters by the concatenate command, concat. This command is used when you wish to put together two strings of characters. It is very useful when it comes to displaying messages and variables together. We shall see both of these commands frequently throughout the text.

Many other formulas may be derived from algebraic equations, but the truth is, this is not done. Computers usually have one code that is used for solving equations instead of many formulas programmed. This saves tremendous time, effort and memory in a computer. For additional practice in developing your style and familiarity with MySQL syntax I offer the following exercises.

1. Write a stored procedure to solve the following equation: $a\sqrt{bx+c}+d = f$, where a, b, c, d and f are constants and x is the variable. Be careful of domain restrictions to insure the equation would exist as a real quantity.

2. Write a stored procedure to solve the following equation: $\dfrac{a}{x+b} = \dfrac{c}{x+d}$ where a, b, c and d are constants and x is the variable. Be careful of domain restrictions to insure the equation would exist as a real quantity.

3. Write a stored procedure to solve the following equation: $a|bx+c|+d = f$ where a, b, c, d and f are constants and x is the variable. Be careful of domain restrictions to insure the equation would exist as a real quantity.

Each of these exercises ask you to keep in mind restrictions of solution sets to insure existence. While coding a formula is usually straightforward, the domain of such formulas must be taken into account in order to provide a complete description of solutions. It is often encouraged to provide quick and informative error messages to let the user know there is a problem. Also, comments in programs help others who are examining or using your code to gain your insight as to what segments of code are doing, so again I encourage this practice as well.

3.2 Factoring

Another major concept covered in an introductory algebra class is factoring natural numbers. This simple concept has profound applications in computer programming, especially in cryptography. There are many advanced algorithms for factoring extremely large numbers, but we shall generate a simple one. This is not the most efficient as it is exhaustive for all integers less than or equal to $\sqrt{n}$. There is a theorem from algebra that states the $\sqrt{n}$ may be used as a stopping condition for determining factors, see for example [5].

```
Delimiter \\
create procedure FactorInteger(
in n int)
Begin
proc_label: Begin
```

```
If n <= 1 then
select 'Error: input must be a positive integer greater than 1'
      as Error_Message;
leave proc_label;
end if;
create temporary table FactorList(factor1 int, factor2 int);
set @i = 1;
while @i <= sqrt(n) do
If floor(n/@i) - n/@i = 0 then
insert into FactorList(factor1, factor2)
values (@i, n/@i);
end if;
set @i = @i + 1;
end while;
end;
end\\
Delimiter ;
call FactorInteger(132);
select * from FactorList;

drop procedure FactorInteger;
drop temporary table FactorList;
```

This procedure has a **leave** command. I use this command if the user input is bad; bad enough in my opinion to warrent re-entering the input value. The procedure will output the error message when you only execute the call command for the stored procedure. If you highlight both the call command line and the select command line the program will continue to run and may give erroneous results, but there will be two result windows in the output display. One will contain the error message and the other will contain the output from running the procedure.

Notice the input variable is of integer type. This allows us to enter values like 13.2 and have them treated like 13. Be careful when using this. If you want to output messages about erroneous input, change the data type in your input variable to **float** or **decimal** and add the following to the if statement: *floor(n) - n <> 0* as a condition. This will output messages about non-integer input. Let's see if we can expand on this procedure.

1. Expand on the FactorInteger procedure to output only the prime factors rather than all the factors.

2. Use the Euclidean Algorithm to write a stored procedure for the greatest common divisor between two positive integers.

3. Write a stored procedure to determine the least common multiple between two positive integers.

4. Write a stored procedure to convert a number to scientific notation.

Chapter 4

College Algebra and Precalculus

College algebra and precalculus courses offer a tremendous amount of material for us to practice with when it comes to stored procedures. This material ranges from formulas from analytic geometry to analysis of polynomials and rational functions to conic sections. Much of the material learned in these courses is automated by some form of technology nowadays. This particular chapter is divided into several sections and they are listed below.

1. Analytic Geometry

2. Polynomial Theory

3. Analysis of Rational Functions

4. Exponential and Logarithms

5. Trigonometry

6. Conic Sections

In each of these sections, we shall see a simple example of a stored procedure and then some explorations into more diverse and slightly more complicated concepts so that you may begin to build your foundation and find your own style of programming in MySQL.

4.1 Analytic Geometry

Analytic geometry is a combination of algebra and analysis applied to geometry. A person's first exposure to analytic geometry usually involves plotting points and analyzing graphs of functions. In the mix of this is usually the distance and midpoint formulas. Below is a stored procedure for determining the distance between two points in the Cartesian coordinate system.

```
Delimiter \\
Create procedure distance(
in x1 float,
in y1 float,
in x2 float,
in y2 float,
out distance float)
begin
set distance = sqrt(pow(x1 - x2, 2) + pow(y1 - y2, 2));
end\\
Delimiter ;
```

Below is a stored procedure for determining the midpoint of a line segment. Keep in mind this is not the only way to do this calculation.

```
Delimiter \\
create procedure Midpoint(
in x1 float,
in y1 float,
in x2 float,
in y2 float)
begin
create temporary table midpointcoord( x float, y float);
insert into midpointcoord(xmid, ymid)
values (0.5 *(x1 + x2), 0.5 *(y1 + y2));
end\\
Delimiter ;
```

The last procedure introduced here is about plotting functions. Since MySQL does not have a built in graphics generator, we would need to generate the points directly and then copy the information to a program that has graphing capability, like Excel, Geogebra or Maple. If we wish to plot a simple curve, we may use the following procedure. This procedure has the function

$$f(x) = \frac{e^{\sqrt{x^2-4}}}{2\pi} \ln(x-1)$$

hard coded for demonstration purposes.

```
/*This procedure will create a
list of (x,y) coordinates that
can be copied into Excel, for
example, to see a plot of a
curve.*/
```

```
Delimiter \\
create procedure plotting(
in n int,
```

```
in xstart float,
in xstop float)
Begin
set @h = (abs(xstop - xstart))/n;
set @i = 0;
create temporary table xycoords(xcoord float, ycoord float);
while @i <= n do
set @x = xstart + @i *@h;
set @y = exp(sqrt(pow(@x,2) - 4))/(2*pi())* ln(@x-1);
/*function hard-coded here!*/
insert into xycoords(xcoord, ycoord)
values(@x, @y);
set @i = @i+1;
end while;
end \\
Delimiter ;
call plotting(20,2,5);
select * from xycoords;
```

This generated a sequence of points that may now be copied to a program capable of plotting lists. The table is given below.

xcoord	ycoord
2	0
2.15	0.0489623
2.3	0.130014
2.45	0.243457
2.6	0.393936
2.75	0.588062
2.9	0.834209
3.05	1.14263
3.2	1.52569
3.35	1.99822
3.5	2.57792
3.65	3.28587
3.8	4.14711
3.95	5.19137
4.1	6.45391
4.25	7.97648
4.4	9.80848
4.55	12.0084
4.7	14.6452
4.85	17.8005
5	21.5706

1. Generalize the stored procedure for the distance formula to handle points

in three dimensions rather than two.

2. Generalize the midpoint formula to find the location of a point on a line segment that is m/n^{th} the way from one endpoint.

4.2 Polynomial Theory

Polynomial theory in college algebra usually falls into two major categories, computational results and behavioral results. Computational results, like the Rational Zero Theorem, Number of Zeros Theorem, Bounds on Zeros Theorem and the Remainder Theorem are mainly prescribing a calculation to perform or their ideas are the result of some computation that has been noted. Behavioral results, like the Tail-End Test, Fundamental Theorem of Algebra and Factor Theorem are those that simply allow us to examine a polynomial and extract information from it. No real computations are involved. Descartes' Rule of Sign is a combination of these two. We may examine a polynomial's coefficients and determine the maximum number of positive or negative real solutions, but then we perform subtractions to capture all possibilities. The good news for us is that practically all computational theorems can be programmed and even some of the behavioral ones may be programmed as well. Believe it, because I'm about to show you, that many of the polynomial theorems can be programmed into a computer. We just have to understand how to make that happen. One of the first theorems encountered in the study of polynomial theory is the Remainder Theorem. How can we make this theorem into a working stored procedure? Below is one way this can be done.

```
Delimiter \\
create procedure RemainderThm(
in x float,
out r float)
Begin
/* function x^2 - 2x - 17 is hard-coded */
set r = pow(x,2) - 2*x - 17;
if r <> 0 then
select 'Value is not a factor' as 'Result Message';
else
select 'Value is a factor' as 'Result Message';
end if;
end \\
Delimiter ;
```

When we consider more behavioral results we may take a different approach. Since most of these are based on the degree of a polynomial or the coefficients, there are ways of reporting results at once. Below is a stored procedure to get you started. I encourage that you add more to this.

```
Delimiter \\
create procedure PolyNotes()
Begin

/*Enter in coefficients of polynomials with the
associated powers on the variable */

create temporary table polylist(exponent int, a float);
insert into polylist(exponent,a)
values(4,1),(3,2),(2,3),(1,4),(0,-5);
set @deg = (select max(exponent) from polylist);
select concat('Number of solutions is ',cast(@deg as char))
    as 'Number of Solutions Message';
set @lead = (select a from polylist where exponent = @deg);
set @const = (select a from polylist where exponent = 0);

/*Tail End Test */

if (floor(@deg/2.0) - @deg/2.0 <> 0 and @lead > 0)  then
select 'Graph starts in Quad III and ends in Quad I'
    as 'Tail End Message';
end if;

if (floor(@deg/2.0) - @deg/2.0 <> 0 and @lead < 0) then
select 'Graph starts in Quad II and ends in Quad IV'
    as 'Tail End Message';
end if;
if (floor(@deg/2.0) - @deg/2.0 = 0 and @lead > 0) then
select 'Graph starts in Quad II and ends in Quad I'
    as 'Tail End Message';
end if;
if (floor(@deg/2.0) - @deg/2.0 = 0 and @lead < 0) then
select 'Graph starts in Quad III and ends in Quad IV'
    as 'Tail End Message';
end if;

/*Cauchy Bounds Theorem */

set @m = (select max(abs(a)) from polylist);
set @bound = 1.0 + @m/abs(@lead);
select concat('All solutions in disc of radius ',
    cast(@bound as char)) as 'Bounds on Roots Message';

/*y-intercept info*/

select concat('y-intercept value is ',
```

```
    cast(@const as char)) as 'Y Intercept Message';
end \\
Delimiter ;
call PolyNotes();
```

This particular procedure is different from the others in that there are neither input nor output variables. Also, we simply call the procedure to see the results from the list we entered in separate tabs. The list entered in as a temporary list is for the coefficients in the order of descending powers. Let's put our stored procedure chops to work now. See if you can tackle these concepts:

1. Write a stored procedure for the Rational Zero Theorem.

2. Write a stored procedure for Descartes' Rule of Sign.

3. For the ambitious: Write a stored procedure for Eisenstein's Criteria. See [5] for a statement of this criteria.

4.3   Rational Functions

The rational function provides strong foundations in complex analysis when dealing with poles and essential singularities. Unfortunately, these topics are not discussed rigorously until after analysis is also well understood. In college algebra and precalculus courses, the primary focus of rational functions are the asymptotes. Horizontal asymptotes are easy to program as they are merely the ratio of leading coefficients, so see if you can write a procedure for this calculation. Vertical asymptotes require a solving procedure. Most solving procedures require calculus notions (specifically Newton's Algorithm which is shown in the Calculus chapter), but we can at least begin with a solving procedure based on the Intermediate Value Theorem, the Bisection Method. This is provided below.

```
Delimiter \\
create procedure Bisection(
in a float,
in b float,
in tol float,
in M int)
proc_label: Begin
set @i = 1;
while @i <= M do
 set @p = a + (b-a)/2.0;

   /* hard coded sqrt(x + 7)-2 into code */

set @z = sqrt(@p + 7.0) - 2.0;
```

```
if (@z = 0 or (b-a)/2.0 < tol) then
select concat('Solution is approximately ', cast(@p as char))
    as Message;
leave proc_label;
end if;
set @i = @i + 1;
if (sqrt(a + 7.0) - 2.0)*(sqrt(@p + 7.0) - 2.0) > 0 then
set a = @p;
else
set b = @p;
end if;
end while;
if @i >= M then
select 'Root not found in interval or number of iterations'
    as Message;
end if;
end\\
Delimiter ;
```

Vertical asymptotes are the roots to the denominator that are distinct from the roots of the numerator (or roots that have a higher multiplicity in the denominator than in the numerator). Using the Bisection Method you may find roots for the denominator. Comparing the multiplicity of the roots is enough to determine if it is indeed a hole or a vertical asymptote. When determining oblique asymptotes, linear divisors are usually the only ones employed in college algebra so the process of synthetic division can be applied. Because of this, I offer the following procedure for synthetic division.

```
Delimiter \\
create procedure SynDiv(
in x0 float)
Begin
create temporary table Poly(i int auto_increment primary key,
    Term varchar(20), Coeff float);
insert into Poly(Term, Coeff)
values('constant', -4),('x-term', 3),('x^2-term', -3),
('x^3-term', 0), ('x^4-term',2);
create temporary table QuoCoeff(j int auto_increment primary key,
    newcoeff float);
set @n = (select count(coeff) from Poly);
set @j = @n-1;
set @y = (select coeff from Poly where i = @n);
insert into QuoCoeff(newcoeff)
values(@y);
while @j > 0 do
set @q = (select Coeff from Poly where i = @j);
set @y = x0*@y + @q;
```

```
insert into QuoCoeff(newcoeff)
values(@y);
set @j = @j - 1;
end while;
end\\
Delimiter ;
call SynDiv(-2);
select * from QuoCoeff;
```

Executing the call command and the following select command yields the following

j	newcoeff
1	2
2	-4
3	5
4	-7
5	10

Note the order of the coefficients in the synthetic division tableau and the corresponding order as a result of the procedure. The last value listed in the table corresponds to the remainder term. This is how the results are to be interpreted.

$$
\begin{array}{r|rrrrr}
 & 2 & 0 & -3 & 3 & -4 \\
-2 & & -4 & 8 & -10 & 14 \\
\hline
 & 2 & -4 & 5 & -7 & 10 \\
\end{array}
$$

A few things are worth mentioning at this point. One is there is a theorem sometimes introduced in college algebra and precalculus that suggest the results of synthetic division can be used to determine bounds on the real roots of polynomials. For example, such a theorem suggests for our particular example here, -2 is a lower bound for the real solutions of the polynomial $2x^4 - 3x^2 + 3x - 4$ since the signs alternate in the coefficients of the quotient and the value we tested was negative. It is also worth mentioning in 2003, Lianghuo Fan published a generalization of the process to include n-th degree polynomials as divisors, see [4].

This procedure uses two new commands, the **auto_increment** and the **primary key** commands. The **auto_increment** command acts like a counter and automatically counts the number of rows as they are added to the table. The **primary key** is a necessary add-on when using the **auto_increment** command. A **primary key** is a column that provides each row with a unique index. You may read more on this topic online or in manuals.

While there are other aspects of rational functions that are explored in these courses, the asymptotes are usually the primary focus. Holes are treated rigorously by some authors, but not others. Specific applications involving rational functions can also be programmed and we have seen a multitude of examples of this. Continuing to add to your portfolio of procedures, see if you can write ones for the following:

1. The acturial method for computing unearned interest.

2. Minimum surface area of a can based on radius.

3. Average cost when provided a cost function. Consult textbooks for sample functions to code into your procedure.

4. Concentration of drugs in a patient's bloodstream. Consult textbooks for sample functions to code into your procedure.

4.4 Logarithms and Exponentials

From the chapter on Introductory Algebra we saw a blueprint for how to write stored procedures for solution formulas, specifically for solving linear and quadratic equations. You were also asked to generate stored procedures for different types that are common in an introductory algebra course. Rather than repeat that same type of discussion, although I definitely encourage you build procedures for solving equations involving logarithms and exponential functions for additional practice, we are going to take on a more applied approach. We shall examine other results common within this topic such as financial applications and population models.

We begin with the change of base formula for logarithms. Because of the rather severe restrictions on the change of base formula for logarithms, I have written breaks in the code. So if an input is erroneous, the procedure will identify the issue and report it to the user.

```
Delimiter \\
create procedure change_of_base(
in M float,
in oldbase float)
begin
proc_label: begin
set @val = NULL;

/*Error checking of inputs, break procedure when
 inputs are nonpositive*/

If oldbase = 1.0 then
select 'Error: base must not be equal to one'
       as Error_Message;
```

```
leave proc_label;
end if;
If (M <= 0 or oldbase <= 0) then
select 'Error: inputs must be strictly positive'
        as Error_Message;
leave proc_label;
else
set @val = ln(M)/ln(oldbase) ;
end if;
end;
end\\
Delimiter ;
```

MySQL has its own change of base command, you may use **select Log(M,x)**
where M is the base to use and x is the input into the logarithm. Some special
logarithms like **Log10(x)** and **Log2(x)** are available. The same restrictions
that are discussed in mathematics courses still apply.

Some popular applications involving exponential and logarithmic functions in
college algebra and precalculus are the population models and financial models
involving annuities. Below is a stored procedure for obtaining results about the
logistic function. I choose the logistic function because there are many prop-
erties discussed in college algebra or precalculus courses concerning the logistic
function. Many of these concepts are relatively new to students and computing
them can be difficult. The standard logistic function appears as

$$P(x) = \frac{a}{1 + be^{-cx}}$$

where a, b and c are parameters into the function, x is the variable, usually
representing time and e is the value $2.718128\ldots$

```
Delimiter \\
create procedure Logistic(
in a float,
in b float,
in c float,
in x float)
Begin
create temporary table LogTable(logistic_value float,
        Description varchar(100));
insert into LogTable(logistic_value, Description)
values (a , 'Carrying Capacity'),
(a/(1+b), 'y-intercept value'),
(NULL, 'x-intercept value'),
(ln(b)/c, 'x-coordinate of inflection point'),
(a/2.0, 'y-coordinate of inflection point'),
(0, 'Horizontal asymptote as x decreases'),
```

```
(a, 'Horizontal asymptote as x increases'),
(-1.0/c*ln((a/x -1)/b),
      concat( 'Time it takes to reach Population size of ',
              cast(x as char)));
end\\
Delimiter ;
```

There are no comments or error checking in this procedure so I encourage you to add these items to this procedure. If you examine some of the formulas you can note some necessary restrictions. This formula also assumes the initial population is less than the carrying capacity and that the population grows over time. Remember these assumptions as you are adding to this procedure. The last line in this table assumes that the input value x is the population and the formula provided specifies the amount of time needed to reach this population. This is a popular question in courses so I include it here.

Compound interest and annuities are common financial formulas found in many texts, not just college algebra or precalculus texts. Many current graphing calculators already have functions programmed in to compute these results. Compound interest also provides good practice for stored procedures (there are several types, future value, present value and continuously compounding) and this a great opportunity for you to show off your programming chops.

Annuities also prove to be a great opportunity, and I will start this one. Below is a procedure for annuities, both ordinary and annuity due. The procedure below is confined to providing results for future values.

```
Delimiter \\
create procedure Annuity(
in R float,
in rate float,
in n int,
in timeframe float,
in paytime varchar(5))
begin
proc_label: Begin
if R <= 0 then
select 'Error: Payments must be made'
      as Error_Message;
leave proc_label;
end if;
if (rate <= 0 or rate >= 1) then
select 'Error: Interest must be in interval (0,1)'
       as Error_Message;
leave proc_label;
end if;
if (floor(n) - n <> 0 or n <= 0 ) then
```

```
select 'Error: Number of periods per year must be
     a positive integer' as Error_message;
leave proc_label;
end if;
if timeframe <= 0 then
select 'Error: Time must be a positive value' as Error_Message;
leave proc_label;
end if;
set @i = rate/n;
set @t = 1.0*n*timeframe;
case paytime when 'Begin' then
set @S = R * ((pow(1 + @i, @t+1) - 1)/@i)-R;
when 'End' then
set @S = R * ((pow(1+@i,@t) - 1)/@i);
end case;
end;
end \\
Delimiter \\
```

This procedure has a **case** command. The use of **case** as opposed to **if** is often a subject for debate among programmers. I used it here to demonstrate a new command to add to your list. As you can see, the case command has a structure all its own for determining a course of action. See if you can decipher this command to learn how to use it properly. Then you can take a side in the "case vs. if" debate.

One of the more involved tasks under annuities is the amortization table. Because we would be producing a table, MySQL is perfectly suited for such a production. Below I offer a procedure to produce such a table.

```
Delimiter \\
create procedure amortization(
in N int,
in loanamt float,
in rate float)
proc_label: Begin
if (floor(N) - N <> 0 or N <=0) then
select 'Error: Number of Payments must be a positive integer'
       as Error_Message;
leave proc_label;
end if;
if loanamt <= 0 then
select 'Error: Amount of loan must be positive' as Error_Message;
leave proc_label;
end if;
if rate <=0 then
select 'Error: Rate must be positive' as Error_Message;
```

```
leave proc_label;
end if;
set @j = 1;
set @i = rate/N;
set @A = loanamt * @i/(1.0 - pow((1.0 + @i),-N));
set @interest = loanamt * @i;
set @newloan = loanamt;
create temporary table Amort(payment_number int,
   Amt_of_Payment float, Interest_of_Payment float,
   Portion_to_Principal float, Loan_Amt float);
insert into Amort(payment_number, Amt_of_Payment,
Interest_of_Payment, Portion_to_Principal, Loan_Amt)
values(0, 0, 0, 0, loanamt);
while @j <= N do
set @interest = @newloan * @i;
set @portion = @A - @interest;
set @newloan = @newloan - @portion;
insert into Amort(payment_number, Amt_of_Payment,
Interest_of_Payment, Portion_to_Principal, Loan_Amt)
values( @j, round(@A,2), round(@interest,2), round(@portion,2),
       abs(round(@newloan,2)));
set @j = @j + 1;
end while;
end\\
Delimiter ;
call amortization(12, 1000, 0.12);
select * from Amort;
select round(sum(Amt_of_Payment),2) as 'Total Amount Paid',
    round(sum(Interest_of_Payment,2) as 'Total Interest Paid'
  from Amort;
```

I include an extra select command here because in many cases the sum of the payments and the amount of interest paid on the loan are often of interest. See if you can tackle these problems.

1. Write a procedure to compute future value and present value of an account with compound or continuously compounding interest. See if you can generate one procedure for all cases rather than four separate procedures.

2. Write a procedure to compute information concerning the Mathusian model (uninhibited growth) for populations, similar to our logistic model procedure.

3. Add to the Annuity procedure the ability to compute the following:

    a) the present value formulas,

    b) the ability to determine the interest rate, and

c) the ability to determine the number of compounding periods.

The Texas Instruments guidebook for their TI-83/84 calculators provides formulas they use and I encourage you to refer to this if you need help determining such formulas.

4. Using the formula below, generate a table for Annual Percentage Rate, APR. Make sure you have appropriate column and row headers involved as well.

$$\textbf{Finance Charge per \$100 Financed} = \frac{100ni}{1 - (1+i)^{-n}} - 100$$

where n is the number of periods and i is the rate divided by 12.

4.5 Trigonometry

Trigonometry is usually the major topic where college algebra and precalculus diverge. This section is here to introduce you to the trigonometric functions that are already programmed in MySQL and to use them when necessary in stored procedures. The first concept introduced under such a topic are the different measurements: degrees, radians and revolutions. Below is a stored procedure for converting one measurement to the other two.

```
Delimiter \\
create procedure DegConvert(
in x float,
in measure varchar(30))
Begin
create temporary table convertto(degrees float, radians float,
        revolutions float);
case measure when 'Degree' then
 insert into convertto(degrees, radians, revolutions)
 values (x, x * Pi()/180, x/360);
 when 'Radians' then
  insert into convertto(degrees, radians, revolutions)
 values (x * 180/Pi(), x, x/(2*Pi()));
  when 'Revolutions' then
   insert into convertto(degrees, radians, revolutions)
 values (x *360, x*2*Pi(),x);
 end case;
 end\\
Delimiter ;
```

Notice this procedure has the ability to accept both numerical and string values as input. In the logistic example, we merely output descriptions as string characters, but here we are actually informing MySQL what type of measurement is being used, either degrees, radians or revolutions. The procedure will output the other two measures accordingly. The **radians()** command will convert degree measurements to radian measure and the **degrees()** command will convert radian measurements to degrees, so you may check your results to make sure this works correctly.

What happens if you want Degrees-Minutes-Seconds instead? The following query (not procedure) will convert Degree measurements to DMS format. I use a degree measurement of 127.567. Also the * is used in place of the usual degree symbol ° for clarity. Feel free to replace this as you see fit. See if you can make this into a procedure.

```
set @xyz = cast(floor(121.567) as char);
set @abc = cast(truncate(121.567 - 121,1)*60 as char(2));
set @def = cast(60*truncate(121.567 - truncate(121.567,1),2)
    as char);
select concat(@xyz ,'* ' ,@abc , '' ' , @def , ' " ');
```

The output of this query is

```
121* 30' 3.60 "
```

When trigonometry is introduced initially, it is done using right triangles. The reasons for this abounds by instructor, but for the most part, it just easy to remember the relationship (SOH-COH-TOA) and it provides a nice graphic which has proven itself many times over to be useful when needed. I offer a chance for you to write a procedure to produce the six basic trigonometric results. Think about this as you write it though, "Do I really need all six to be produced or do I want to give the user the choice?" See if you can do it both ways. MySQL has four trigonometric functions programmed in already.

Trig function	MySQL command
sine	sin()
cosine	cos()
tangent	tan()
cotangent	cot()

Notice MySQL does not have functions defined for secant or cosecant. You will have to use the definitions directly to generate those functions. If you are generating functions for any angle, not just those confined to right triangles, watch out for domains as well. Different textbooks will define the domain differently based on need and convenience.

Unit circle trigonometry usually follows as an extension of right triangle trigonometry. They work hand-in-hand actually and you can interchange which one comes first. A task for you is to reproduce the usual unit circle charts seen in precalculus texts. You have the tools and here is a chance for you to continue to develop your own style.

Inverse trigonometry is usually a pesky topic in trigonometry. MySQL has some inverse trigonometric functions available for use directly. There are many applications where inverse trigonometry is used. MySQL has the following inverse trigonometric functions:

Inverse trig function	MySQL command
arcsine	asin()
arccosine	acos()
arctangent	atan()

Note the other inverse trigonometric functions are not defined. The inverse secant and inverse cosecant functions usually have different definitions of their domain based on authorship. When asked in the Exercises, you will have to make a decision about the domain of these functions and also make a note for other potential users to let them know the domain you are using.

Vectors are usually another pesky topic for students in precalculus. Since MySQL is typically used for databases, we may consider a vector as a single-column table. Below is a stored procedure for the *dot product*, also known as the *inner product*.

```
Delimiter \\
create procedure DotProduct()
proc_label: Begin
create temporary table vector1(location int, entries1 float);
insert into vector1(location, entries1)
values(1,1),(2,2),(3,3);
create temporary table vector2(location int, entries2 float);
insert into vector2(location, entries2)
values(1,5),(2,-4),(3,2);
set @n = (select count(entries1) from vector1);
set @m = (select count(entries2) from vector2);
set @i = 1;
if @n = @m then
set @p = ( select sum(vector1.entries1 * vector2.entries2)
from vector1, vector2
where vector1.location = vector2.location);
else
select 'Error: Vector Lengths must be equal' as 'Error Message';
leave proc_label;
end if;
if @p = 0 then
select 'Vectors are orthogonal' as Message;
end if;
end\\
```

```
Delimiter ;
```

The magnitude and direction of a vector are also common calculations when vectors are first introduced. Here is a procedure for determining the magnitude and direction of a single two-dimensional vector.

```
Delimiter \\
create procedure magdirection(
in xcomp float,
in ycomp float,
out mag float)
begin
set mag = sqrt(pow(xcomp,2) + pow(ycomp,2));
if mag = 0 then
select 'Zero vector has no direction' as Message;
else
create temporary table vectdirect(magnitude float, comp1 float,
        comp2 float);
insert into vectdirect
values(mag, xcomp/mag,ycomp/mag);
end if;
end\\
Delimiter ;
```

The last pieces of the puzzle in introductory trigonometry are the Law of Sines and the Law of Cosines. I leave the Law of Sines for you to write and provide a Law of Cosines procedure below. I added comments to help explain how the procedure works. Also, since inputs can vary in position, the resulting table explains which part of the triangle the result is associated with. If you use this, pay attention to how you enter the information since the resulting comments are related to the order the numbers are entered.

```
/* ********************************
/* Triangle type refers to SSS or SAS. If you
/* choose SSS, then the three numbers input
/* represent the sides of the triangle. If you
/* choose SAS then the second input represents
/* degree measurement of angle. The procedure
/* will automatically convert to radians.
********************************/
Delimiter \\
create procedure LawofCosines(
in a float,
in b float,
in c float,
in triangletype char(3))
```

```
proc_label: Begin
create temporary table Results(ans1 varchar(100), ans2
   varchar(100), ans3 varchar(100));
case triangletype when 'SAS' then
if (a <= 0 or c <= 0) then
select 'Error: Sides must be positive lengths.' as 'Error Message';
leave proc_label;
end if;
if b <= 0 then
select 'Error: Angle must be a positive measure.'
   as 'Error Message';
leave proc_label;
end if;

/*angle conversion */

set @theta = b * Pi()/180;
set @c2 = pow(a,2) + pow(c,2) - 2*a*c*cos(@theta);
set @angle2 = 180/Pi() * acos((pow(c,2) - pow(a,2) - @c2)/
      (-2*a*sqrt(@c2)));
set @angle3 = 180 - b - @angle2;
insert into Results(ans1, ans2, ans3)
values (sqrt(@c2), @angle2, @angle3),
('missing side','angle opposite
      last-entered side', 'last missing angle');

when 'SSS' then
if (a <= 0 or b <= 0 or c <= 0) then
select 'Error: Sides must be positive lengths.' as 'Error Message';
leave proc_label;
end if;
set @angle1 = 180/Pi() * (acos((pow(c,2) - pow(a,2) -
   pow(b,2))/(-2*a*b)));
set @angle2 = 180/Pi() * (acos((pow(b,2) - pow(a,2) -
   pow(c,2))/(-2*a*c)));
set @angle3 = 180 - @angle1 - @angle2;
insert into Results(ans1, ans2, ans3)
values (@angle1, @angle2, @angle3),
('angle opposite last-entered side','angle opposite
      middle-entered side','angle opposite first-entered side');
end case;
end \\
Delimiter ;
```

Try the following exercises.

  1. Write a stored procedure for the Law of Sines.

2. Write a stored procedure for computing linear speed from angular speed, include the ability to handle problems measured in degrees, radians or revolutions.

3. Write a stored procedure for the three inverse trigonometric functions that are not already available in MySQL.

4. Write a stored procedure for solving this problem:

   An airplane has an airspeed of 200 miles per hour in a direction due north. The wind velocity is 45 miles per hour in a southwesterly direction. Find the actual speed and direction of the plane relative to the ground.

   Keep the inputs general so you may use this procedure to solve other problems of this type.

5. One particular set of calculations associated with vectors are the parallel and perpendicular components. Write a stored procedure that produces these values for a three-dimensional vector. Note that if the z-direction is 0 for both vectors, it will be a two-dimensional result.

4.6 Conic Sections

In this last section, I provide a stored procedure for obtaining information about an ellipse. I do this so you may use this as a blueprint for resolving the other two conic sections. This stored procedure assumes the ellipse is in standard form:

$$\frac{(x-h)^2}{a^2} + \frac{(y-k)^2}{b^2} = 1$$

```
Delimiter \\
create procedure ellipse(
in a float,
in b float,
in h float,
in k float)
proc_label: Begin
if (a <= 0 or b <= 0) then
select 'Error: Distances must be positive values' as Error_Message;
leave proc_label;
end if;
set @c = sqrt(greatest(pow(a,2),pow(b,2)) - least(pow(a,2),
    pow(b,2)));
create temporary table ELLTable(Result float, Description
    varchar(100));
if pow(a,2) > pow(b,2) then
insert into ELLTable(Result, Description)
```

```
values(h, 'x-coordinate of center'),
(k, 'y-coordinate of center'),
(h + @c, 'x-coordinate of focus 1'),
(h - @c, 'x-coordiante of focus 2'),
(NULL, 'traverse axis parallel to x-axis'),
(h + a, 'x-coordinate of vertex 1'),
(h - a, 'x -coordinate of vertex 2'),
(k, 'y-coordinate of vertices and foci'),
(2*pow(b,2)/a, 'length of focal chord'),
(2*b, 'length of minor axis'),
(2*a, 'length of major axis'),
(@c/a, 'eccentricity'),
(h - pow(a,2)/@c , 'Vertical Directrix 1'),
(h + pow(a,2)/@c, 'Vertical Directrix 2');
else
insert into ELLTable(Result, Description)
values(h, 'x-coordinate of center'),
(k, 'y-coordinate of center'),
(k + @c, 'y-coordinate of focus 1'),
(k - @c, 'y-coordiante of focus 2'),
(NULL, 'traverse axis parallel to y-axis'),
(k + a, 'y-coordinate of vertex 1'),
(k - a, 'y -coordinate of vertex 2'),
(h, 'x-coordinate of vertices and foci'),
(2*pow(b,2)/a, 'length of focal chord'),
(2*b, 'length of major axis'),
(2*a, 'length of minor axis'),
(@c/b, 'eccentricity'),
(k - pow(b,2)/@c , 'Horizontal Directrix 1'),
(k + pow(b,2)/@c, 'Horizontal Directrix 2');
end if;
end \\
Delimiter ;
```

The last exercise asks you to write a stored procedure to accomodate general form of a conic: $Ax^2 + Bxy + Cy^2 + Dx + Ey + F = 0$. Making one procedure that is more dynamic than three geared for a specific conic section is much more desirable. Remember the more dynamic stored procedures are and the more general they are, usually the better and by now I believe you have the expertise to take this task on. You can do it!

1. Write stored procedures for the hyperbola and parabola. Display the common information as was done with the ellipse stored procedure.

2. Write a stored procedure to obtain at least twenty points of a conic section when using the polar forms. Remember to keep this to one procedure for all conic sections.

3. Write a stored procedure to produce the hyperbolic and inverse hyperbolic trigonometric functions. Try to keep it to one procedure for hyperbolic trigonometric functions and one procedure for the inverse hyperbolic trigonometric functions. The procedure can return just the value of the function with an input value that is a member of the domain. An error message should be returned if the input value is not in the domain.

4. Write a stored procedure to produce the basic information for a conic section but use the general formula, $Ax^2 + Bxy + Cy^2 + Dx + Ey + F = 0$ and include the angle of rotation. Try to keep it to one procedure.

Chapter 5

Calculus

In this chapter we tackle common concepts in calculus and apply some numerical techniques for approximating results. It is very important to remember that MySQL is not designed for hardcore mathematical numerical analysis. It has basic mathematics functions already programmed in, but when it comes to stored procedures, you will most likely be hard coding the functions into the stored procedures. That is because it does not have a computer algebra system available like *Maple* and *Mathematica* do. These concepts include:

1. Limits

2. Differentiation

3. Integration

4. Sequences and Series

5. Vector Calculus

5.1 Limits

A limit is the first real calculus concept introduced to students. To numerically apply a limit calculation requires the use of the $\epsilon - \delta$ definition since it is not a substitution. We review this definition below.

Definition of Limit Let $f(x)$ be defined on an open interval containing a, except possibly at a itself. The **limit** as x approaches a of $f(x)$ is the number L, and write

$$\lim_{x \to a} f(x) = L,$$

if, for any given $\epsilon > 0$, there is a corresponding number $\delta > 0$ such that for all x,

$$0 < \left| x - a \right| < \delta \Rightarrow \left| f(x) - L \right| < \epsilon.$$

I demonstrate one way to implement such a definition with MySQL.

```
Delimiter \\
create procedure functionlimit(
in x float,
in epsilon float,
in delta float)
proc_label: Begin

/* A little error protection */

if (epsilon <= 0 or delta <= 0) then
select 'Error: epsilon or delta must be positive values'
   as Error_Message;
leave proc_label;
end if;

/* table to store left and right sided limits
to track progress from both sides*/

create temporary table
limitvals(seqcount int, left_approach float, right_approach float,
   left_fnc float, right_fnc float);
set @N = 100;
set @h = (x - delta)/(@N) ;
set @i = 1;

/*Function 1/sqrt(x^2 + 7) hard-coded in loop */

while @i < @N do
set @x0left = x-(@N - @i)*@h;
set @x0right = x+(@N-@i)*@h;
set @yl = 1.0/(sqrt(pow(@x0left,2) + 7));
set @yr = 1.0/(sqrt(pow(@x0right,2) + 7));
insert into limitvals(seqcount, left_approach, right_approach,
   left_fnc, right_fnc)
values(@i, @x0left, @x0right, @yl, @yr);
if abs(@yl - @yr) < epsilon then
set @L = (@yl + @yr)/2.0;
select @L as 'approx limit';
leave proc_label;
end if;
set @i = @i + 1;
end while;
end \\
Delimiter ;
```

```
call functionlimit(1,0.01,0.1);
select * from limitvals;
```

Notice this procedure only works if the value our inputs approach from the left and right is a finite value. See if you can make modifications to this procedure such that limits toward infinity or negative infinity are able to be computed.

Continuity is also a concept involving limits. The definition of continuity usually involves three criteria:

- The function must exist at the point in question,

- The limit from the left and the limit from the right must equal the full limit, and

- The full limit must equal the function evaluation.

Here are a couple questions about continuity involving our limit procedure.

1. Can the procedure above for limits also be used for continuity? Explain.

2. Write a stored procedure to test for continuity at a point.

5.2 Differentiation

There are many issues associated with differentiation. Most of these issues stem from the fact that differentiation is a local issue, not a global one. Finite differencing is a popular numerical approach to differentiation, but stability and complicated difference quotients become an issue when the order of differentiation becomes large. It is popular because the method stems straight from the definition of derivative and most equations where finite differencing is used do not go beyond order two in the approximation (approximating the second derivative). The finite difference method really is nothing more than the average rate of change and Taylor series expansions evaluated at some point inside an open interval. Central differencing is the most popular due to the error being smaller and the formulas are not too complicated for low order differentiation. Below I offer a stored procedure for the first and second finite difference approximation to the derivative at a point. The TI-83/84 calculator's nDerive command also uses a similar scheme.

```
Delimiter \\
create procedure FiniteDifference(in x float)
begin
set @i = 1;
set @n = 20;
set @h = 1.0;
create temporary table DerApprox(delta float, approx float);
while @i <= @n do
```

```
set @Der = (sqrt(x+0.5*@h) - sqrt(x-0.5*@h))/@h;

/* function sqrt(x) hard-coded */

set @h = pow(0.5,@i);
insert into DerApprox(delta, approx)
values(@h, @Der);
set @i = @i + 1;
end while;
end \\
Delimiter ;
```

The second order finite difference is also provided below. The procedure is essentially the same, except for the computation of the approximation for the second derivative at the specified point.

```
Delimiter \\
create procedure SecondDerivative(in x float)
begin
set @i = 1;
set @n = 20;
set @h = 1.0;
create temporary table SecondDerApprox(delta float, approx float);
while @i <= @n do
set @Der = (sqrt(x+@h) - 2*sqrt(x) + sqrt(x-@h))/pow(@h,2);

/* function sqrt(x) hard-coded */

set @h = pow(0.5,@i);
insert into SecondDerApprox(delta, approx)
values(@h, @Der);
set @i = @i + 1;
end while;
end \\
Delimiter ;
```

Higher order finite difference approximations become more complex with the arithmetic and can lead to instability. If you run these finite differencing schemes for too many iterations, you'll see errroneous results appear. Right now the only stopping condition is after the finite differencing runs for 20 times (@n = 20). If this is increased you may see errors creep into the results. Go ahead and try it, increase @n to say 50 iterations and you'll see the results increase toward infinity. I leave it to you to implement stopping conditions to insure accurate answers are being reported.

One of the first actual numerical schemes introduced to mathematics students is Newton's Method. It is a method used to solve equations. It is often introduced in calculus courses as a useful application of the derivative of the function in question.

```
Delimiter \\
create procedure NewtonsMethod(
in p float,
in tol float,
in N int
)
proc_label: Begin
set @i = 1;

/* Create a table to store approximations from scheme */

create temporary table NewtonTable( j int, approx float);
insert into NewtonTable(j, approx)
values (@i, p);
set @p = p;

/* The function, x^2-x and its derivative,
2x - 1 are hard-coded into the loop */

while @i <= N do
set @q = @p - (pow(@p,2) - @p)/(2.0*@p - 1.0);

/* Here is where the functions are hard-coded */

If abs(@q - @p)  < tol then
leave proc_label;
end if;
set @i = @i + 1;
insert into NewtonTable(j, approx)
values(@i, @q);
set @p = @q;
end while;
end \\
Delimiter ;
```

If you wish, you may attempt to add in a code for computing a derivative at the point in question inside Newton's Method. Right now, this procedure has the derivative function hard-coded.

An alternative to Newton's Method is the Secant Method. The Secant Method avoids the use of the derivative, but loses speed in convergence to a solution. A stored procedure for the Secant Method is given below.

```
Delimiter \\
create procedure secantmethod(
in a float,
in b float,
in tol float,
in M int)
proc_label: Begin

/* Create table to store previous iterations for
display purposes */

create temporary table approxsoln(j int, z float);

/* Initializing inputs. Function hard-coded as cos(x) - x */

set @i = 2;
set @q0 = cos(a) - a;
set @q1 = cos(b) - b;
insert into approxsoln(j, z)
values(0, a );
while @i <= M do
set @q1 = cos(b) - b;
set @pnew = b - @q1*(b - a)/(@q1 - @q0);

/* Stopping condition */

if abs(@pnew - b) <= tol then
leave proc_label;
end if;

/* Updates for next iteration */

insert into approxsoln(j,z)
values(@i-1,@pnew);
set a = b;
set @q0 = @q1;
set b = @pnew;
set @q1 = cos(@pnew) - @pnew;
set @i = @i + 1;
end while;

/* What happens when a solution is not found
   within the number of iterations specified.*/

if (abs(@pnew - b) > tol and @i > M) then
select 'Max iterations reached' as Msg;
```

```
end if;
end\\
Delimiter ;
```

It is common for equation solvers to have approximations stored in tables to see if scheme is actually converging on a solution. While much time is spent solving equations in algebra and precalculus courses, numerical methods involve differentiation and variants of the average rate of change. This is one reason why solving methods are introduced in this chapter rather than in the algebra chapter. These schemes are not dependent on a specific type of equation such as a linear equation, quadratic or exponential equation where you would build formulas for solving if possible. A great test to see if these schemes "work" is to test them against each other on the same equation. You must be careful with the initial points for these schemes, it is known that some initial points for some equations do not yield any results.

1. Consider the following related rates problem:
   Suppose Car A is approaching a right-angled intersection from the south while Car B has already passed the intersection going west. When Car A is 0.5 miles from the intersection and Car B is 0.7 miles from the intersection, it is determined the distance between them is increasing at a rate of 15 miles per hour. If Car A is traveling at 40 mph at the instant of the measurement, what is the speed of Car B?

   See if you can write the stored procedure so any related rates problem involving triangles can be solved.

2. Consider the following optimization problem:
   An open box with a square base is to be constructed from a square piece of steel measuring 48 inches per side. How large should the squares that are cut from the corners be in order to maximize the volume of the box?

   Write the procedure so that any optmization question of this type can be solved via your procedure.

3. Write a procedure for the linearization of functions. Use the following example to test your procedure $f(x) = \sqrt{x+9}$ at $x = 4$. Write the procedure so the values of the derivative are determined via the finite difference method rather than hard-coded.

5.3 Integration

In a course on integral calculus, students are often introduced to the numerical techniques of integration, specifically the Trapezoid Rule and the Simspon Rule. While these techniques are great learning tools for seeing how polynomial approximation can be used to approximate the integral, more powerful techniques are often employed in industry and are based on quadrature methods.

I introduce a procedure for the Trapezoid Rule here applied to the function $y = \dfrac{1}{x}$.

```
Delimiter \\
create procedure TrapezoidRule(
in a float,
in b float,
in n int,
out areaapprox float)
Begin
set @h = (b-a)/n;
set @i = 1;
set @z =0.0;

/*Evaluate left endpoint function value*/

set @leftendvalue  = 1.0/a;

 /*Evaluate right endpoint function value*/

set @rightendvalue  = 1.0/b;

/*Evaluate function values in the interior*/

set @areaapp  = @leftendvalue;
while (@i <= n-1)  do
set @z  = a + @i * @h;
set @areaapp  = @areaapp +  2.0*1.0/@z;
set @i  = @i + 1;
end while;
set @areaapp  = @areaapp + @rightendvalue;
Select 0.5*@h*@areaapp into areaapprox;
end\\
Delimiter ;
```

The Trapezoid Rule is essentially a linear approximation to the curve between nodes. Simpson's rule is a quadratic approximation. This is set up as an exercise for you.

The irony of all this is the fact that industry rarely uses such rules. Quadrature methods are often employed instead because of their accuracy, speed and ability to handle a larger group of functions. Below is a scheme for an introductory Gaussian Quadrature method. A slightly more general technique, the Gauss-Kronrod can be employed. The TI-83/84 calculators use a Gauss-Kronrod scheme for their fInt command.

```
/*This particular quadrature formula is
designed for five zeros of the
Legendre polynomials and associated
weight factors. This is also confined to
the interval [-1,1]. The function is
hard-coded into the procedure.*/
Delimiter \\
create procedure GaussQuad()
Begin
create temporary table LegendreX(Zcounter int,
    legendre_zero float);
insert into LegendreX(Zcounter, Legendre_zero)
values(1, -0.906179845938664),
(2,-0.538469310105683),
(3, 0.0),
(4,0.538469310105683),
(5,0.906179845938664);
create temporary table GaussW(Wcounter int, weighting float);
insert into GaussW(Wcounter, weighting)
values(1, 0.236926885056189),
(2, 0.478628670499366),
(3,0.568888888888889),
(4,0.478628670499366),
(5,0.236926885056189);

/*function e^(-x^2)) hard-coded as function to integrate from -1 to 1*/

create temporary table QuadVals(integral_values float);
set @j = 1;
while @j <= 5 do
insert into QuadVals (integral_values)
 (select   a.weighting*exp(-1.0* pow((b.legendre_zero),2))
     from GaussW a join LegendreX b on a.Wcounter = b.Zcounter
where a.Wcounter = @j and b.Zcounter = @j);
set @j = @j + 1;
end while;
end\\
Delimiter ;
```

This particular code contains a **join** command. This is likely the most used command next to the **select** command in the arsenals of SQL and MySQL. The ability to join tables is at the heart of these languages. It is a vital component of working with databases. There are many types of joins and this is a heavily treated subject when working with SQL or MySQL. If you are using SQL or MySQL on a regular basis in the workplace, it is knowing what it is in the tables that makes you sharp. Coding skills can always be refined, but intimate knowledge of the tables is what makes you work well.

There are many variations of Gaussian Quadrature methods. These methods stem from the ability to approximate functions with polynomials (a result of the Stone-Weierstrass Theorem). Special functions, such as Chebyshev polynomials or Legendre polynomials are often employed for these purposes since they are orthogonal polynomials and relatively easy to generate.

1. Write a stored procedure for Simpson's Rule.

2. Write a stored procedure for Gaussian Quadrature using 12 points instead of 5. See [1], or other online sources for the values of the nodes and roots to Legendre's polynomials needed for this exercise.

3. Write a stored procedure for Romberg Integration.

4. For the ambitious: Write a stored procedure for Gauss-Kronrod Quadrature method. Use online resourses to determine the nodes and weights associated with the method. Fifteen nodes and weights is considered standard in industry, also known as the Gauss Kronrod 7−15 Method.

5.4   Sequences and Series

The ideas of sequences or series form a major portion of the backbone of applied mathematics. Many of the numerical schemes constructed are based on generating sequences of values and then refining the sequence until we obtain the desired result, or establish such results cannot be achieved. No discussion of sequences would be complete without a mention of the famous Fibonacci sequence. This sequence occurs quite often in nature and has many results associated with it. Below is a stored procedure producing values for the Fibonacci sequence. There is an additional column of the ratios of values demonstrating the convergence to the golden ratio.

```
Delimiter \\
create procedure Fibonacci(
in n int)
proc_label: Begin
if (floor(n) - n <> 0 or n <= 3) then
select 'Error: counter must be at least 3 and an integer'
      as Error_Message;
leave proc_label;
end if;
set @a1 = 1;
set @a2 = 1;
set @i = 3;
create temporary table FiboNumbers( counter int,
      Fibo_Number int, ratio float);
```

```
insert into FiboNumbers(counter, Fibo_Number, ratio)
values (1, 1, 1), (2, 1, 1);
while @i <= n do
set @a = @a1 + @a2;
set @x = (select Fibo_Number from FiboNumbers
     where counter = @i - 1);
set @y = (select Fibo_Number from FiboNumbers
     where counter = @i - 2);
insert into FiboNumbers(counter, Fibo_Number, ratio)
values (@i, @a, @x/@y);
set @a2 = @a1;
set @a1 = @a;
set @i = @i + 1;
end while;
end\\
Delimiter ;
```

The additional column, 'ratio' in the FiboNumbers table was an afterthought when I first wrote this stored procedure. I decided to add it in after the fact. It is important that you carefully plan your tables ahead of time so they may be joined with other tables or have the information you wish to have. I am using temporary tables in my procedures and these tables are populated when the procedure runs. This allows me to fix these tables relatively quickly if there is something I wish to add to the table or change the columns in the table. Attempting to change permanent tables after they are created by replacing specific values or adding additional columns is sometimes not worth the effort when careful planning could take care of those inconveniences.

There are many tests to choose from when determining if a sequence or series converges. One of the first tests introduced is the Ratio Test. Below is a stored procedure for the Ratio Test. Other tests, such as the Root Test may also be programmed and I encourage you add this. There are some sequences where the Ratio Test fails and the Root Test may be applied successfully.

```
Delimiter \\
/* Terms in series are 3^n/n!, hard-coded after while loop */
create procedure RatioTest(
in n int)
proc_label: Begin
if (floor(n) - n <> 0 or n <= 0) then
select 'Error: counter must be a positive integer'
    as ' Error Mesage';
leave proc_label;
end if;
set @fact = 1;
set @i = 1;
while @i <= n do
```

```
set @fact = @i *@fact;
set @i = @i + 1;
end while;
set @a = pow(3,n)/@fact;
set @b = pow(3,n+1)/(@fact *(n+1));
set @r = @b/@a;
if @r < 1 then
select 'Series Convergences by Ratio Test' as Result;
elseif @r > 1 then
select 'Series Divergence by Ratio Test' as Result;
else
select 'Test inconclusive' as Result;
end if;
end \\
Delimiter ;
```

This particular stored procedure has an **elseif** command. This command is used similar to an **if-then-else** except it provides the addition of another alternative rather than one condition to be tested as true or false. The elseif command allows pursuit of another course of action if the original statement is false. Also, this particular stored procedure will only return a message, it does not have a table of values to show the ratios as they occur. If you wish, you may alter this procedure to do just that.

1. Write a stored procedure for the Root Test.

2. Write a stored procedure for the geometric sequence and series.

3. Write a stored procedure for arithmetic sequence and series.

4. Write a stored procedure for harmonic sequence and series.

The last three exercises are vague in their instruction. Think about what *you* would like to see if you were inquiring about these sequences or series. Use textbooks to see common questions asked about the sequence or series to help guide you.

5.5   Vector Calculus

Multivariate calculus usually generalizes single variable calculus techniques when it comes to the major topics: limits, derivatives and integrals. One conceptual difference between multivariate and single-variable calculus usually comes with the directional derivative. The good news is that these concepts may be formulated with the help of vectors. So vector calculus offers techniques and formulas that may be more conducive to a programming language such as MySQL. Remember, MySQL is used primarily for databases and vectors may be considered single-column tables. So we shall employ our vector calculus skills. To start we may consider a procedure for computing the directional derivative.

```
Delimiter \\
create procedure DirectionalDerivative(
in x float,
in y float)
proc_label: Begin

/*Direction vector*/

create temporary table directionvector( component int,
        compval float);
insert into directionvector(component, compval)
values(1,3),(2,-4);

/*Partial derivatives of f(x) = xe^y + cos(xy) hard-coded.
These will be evaluated at the point of interest.
@fx represents x-partial derivative
@fy represents y-partial derivative*/

set @fx = exp(y) - y* sin(x*y);
set @fy = x*exp(y) - x*sin(x*y);
create temporary table
partialderivativefunctions( component int, pdfunctionsval float);
insert into partialderivativefunctions(component, pdfunctionsval)
values(1,@fx),(2, @fy);

/* unit vector calculation */

set @mag = (select sqrt(sum(pow(compval,2)))
    from directionvector);
if @mag = 0 then
select 'Zero vector has no direction' as Message;
leave proc_label;
else
create temporary table
        unitdirectionvector(componentdirection int, comp float);
insert into unitdirectionvector(componentdirection, comp)
select a.component, 1/@mag * a.compval from directionvector a;
end if;

/* dot product computation */

set @prod = (select sum(a.pdfunctionsval * b.comp)
from partialderivativefunctions a
```

```
join unitdirectionvector b on a.component = b.componentdirection);
end \\
Delimiter ;
call directionalderivative(2,0);
select @prod as result;
```

Notice this particular procedure has the partial derivatives hard-coded for the example. See if you can modify this process by using a finite difference scheme to approximate the first derivatives of the function. Would this be an improvement in your opinion? Argue your points. The reason why I am asking this is because this is a central point of coding, what should be coded to help the user perform the task and what should the user input based on how the language works. Since MySQL is limited mathematically as far as symbolic manipulations are concerned, do you think it is better to hard-code functions or not?

Vector calculus offers many cases where a procedure may be useful. Two common examples are ideal projectile motion and the TNB frame. First we have a stored procedure for ideal projectile motion. This is merely a collection of formulas to produce answers to common questions.

```
Delimiter \\
create procedure IPM(
in initvelocity float,
in firingangle float,
in timeframe float,
in gravity float)
proc_label: Begin
if timeframe < 0 then
select 'Error: Time must be a nonnegative value' as Error_Message;
leave proc_label;
end if;
If (firingangle <= 0  or firingangle > Pi()/2.0) then
select 'Error: Firing angle must be a positive value in radians'
       as Error_Message;
leave proc_label;
end if;
If gravity <= 0 then
select 'Error: Gravity must be a positive value' as Error_Message;
leave proc_label;
end if;
set @x = initvelocity * cos(firingangle)* timeframe;
set @y = initvelocity * sin(firingangle)*timeframe -
       0.5 * gravity * pow(timeframe,2);
set @R = pow(initvelocity,2)/gravity * sin(2*firingangle);
set @flighttime = 2*initvelocity*sin(firingangle)/gravity;
set @maxheight = 0.5 * pow(initvelocity *
```

```
    sin(firingangle),2)/gravity;
end\\
Delimiter ;
```

Notice this program allows you to select which values you need, it will not output all the values. Do not forget the trigonometric functions in MySQL have default setting to radians. If you are going to use these functions directly, the input values must be in radian measure.

The TNB frame from physics is one of the more daunting calculations that students are asked to examine during a course in vector calculus. Writing a stored procedure for this topic can save hours of frustrating calculations. Below is one such procedure.

```
/* compute the first three derivatives of
the vector function r(t). For our example,
we have  r(t) = <t^2, t, t^3> and the
point of evaluation is t = 2.*/

Delimiter \\
create procedure TNB(
in t float)
proc_label: Begin

/* Creating first three derivatives as vectors */

create temporary table rderive1(compnumber1 int, comp1 float);
create temporary table rderive2(compnumber2 int, comp2 float);
create temporary table rderive3(compnumber3 int, comp3 float);
insert into rderive1(compnumber1, comp1)
values(1,2*t),(2,1),(3,3*pow(t,2));
insert into rderive2(compnumber2, comp2)
values(1,2),(2,0),(3,6*t);
insert into rderive3(compnumber3, comp3)
values(1,0),(2,0),(3,6);
set @s1 = (select sqrt(sum(pow(comp1,2))) from rderive1);
if @s1 = 0 then
select 'Zero vector!' as Message;
leave proc_label;
end if;
update rderive1 set comp1 = comp1/@s1;
set @prod12 = (select sum(b.comp2 * a.comp1) from rderive1 a
join rderive2 b on a.compnumber1 = b.compnumber2);
create temporary table newrderive2(newcompnumber2 int
      auto_increment primary key, newcomp2 float);
insert into newrderive2(newcomp2)
select b.comp2 - @prod12 * a.comp1 from rderive1 a
```

```
join rderive2 b on a.compnumber1 = b.compnumber2;
set @prod13 = (select sum(c.comp3 * a.comp1) from rderive1 a
join rderive3 c on a.compnumber1 = c.compnumber3);
create temporary table newrderive3(newcompnumber3
        int auto_increment primary key, newcomp3 float);
insert into newrderive3 (newcomp3)
select c.comp3 - @prod13 * a.comp1 from rderive1 a
join rderive3 c on a.compnumber1 = c.compnumber3;
set @s2 = (select sqrt(sum(pow(newcomp2,2)))
        from newrderive2);
if @s2 = 0 then
select 'Zero vector!' as Message;
leave proc_label;
end if;
update newrderive2 set newcomp2 = newcomp2/@s2;
set @prod23 = (select sum(c.newcomp3 * b.newcomp2)
        from newrderive2 b
join newrderive3 c on b.newcompnumber2 = c.newcompnumber3);
create temporary table lastrderive3(lastnewcompnumber3 int
        auto_increment primary key, lastnewcomp3 float);
insert into lastrderive3(lastnewcomp3)
select c.newcomp3 - @prod23 * b.newcomp2 from newrderive2 b
join newrderive3 c on b.newcompnumber2 = c.newcompnumber3;
set @s3 = (select sqrt(sum(pow(lastnewcomp3,2)))
   from lastrderive3);
if @s3 = 0 then
select 'Zero vector!' as Message;
leave proc_label;
end if;
update lastrderive3 set lastnewcomp3 = lastnewcomp3/@s3;
end \\
Delimiter ;
call TNB(2);
select a.comp1 as Tangent, b.newcomp2 as Normal,
        c.lastnewcomp3 as Binormal from lastrderive3 c
join newrderive2 b on b.newcompnumber2 = c.lastnewcompnumber3
join  rderive1 a on a.compnumber1 = b.newcompnumber2;
```

For those who had courses in linear algebra, you may notice this is very similar to a Gram-Schmidt orthonormalization process. The original process is numerically unstable, but this scheme is modified slightly to give more stability when computing.

In this particular code, we used a new command. The **update** command was used to normalize the vectors while the process ran. If you are using an update command you may come across this error:

Error Code: 1175. You are using safe update mode and you tried to update a table without a WHERE that uses a KEY column. To disable safe mode, toggle the option in Preferences $-$ > SQL Editor and reconnect.

What this message is trying to tell you is the following:

1. Go under the Edit and select Preferences,

2. Highlight SQL Editor, it is usually next to the first downward pointing arrow,

3. At the bottom of the window, there will be a checkbox with "Safe Updates", uncheck this box and hit OK.

4. Go under the Query Tab and select "Reconnect to Server".

5. Run the procedure again. It should work without this error appearing.

Here we can see the use of the **auto_increment** command and the **primary key** again. See if you can explain why these are here. After the **call** command is executed, we have the joining of the tables to present the results. We have seen joins with two tables, but it is obviously possible to join as many tables as you wish as long as you have a column to join them on. This gives a single command for a clean output.

One thing you may want to keep in mind, and something I was told by my supervisor, is that we want to develop codes and outputs that require a minimum amount of human interaction. Basically, don't do three queries to bring up three small chunks of information, use one query to bring it all together. It takes practice, a lot of it. The more you practice, the more skills you will have. This leads to better communication with others who have more experience with SQL or MySQL and ultimately better coding practices. Keep up the good work!

1. The stored procedure for Ideal Projectile Motion does not include wind gusts. See if you can modify the procedure to account for wind gusts. It also does not account for a starting position other than the origin. See if you can modify the code to accomplish this as well. Keep this to one procedure to capture both these situations simultaneously.

2. Write a stored procedure using finite differencing to compute the following partial derivatives
$$\frac{\partial f}{\partial x}, \frac{\partial f}{\partial y}, \text{ and } \frac{\partial^2 f}{\partial x \partial y}.$$
Research methods to determine which finite difference scheme you'd like to use and explain why.

3. Write a stored procedure to compute the divergence of a vector.

4. Write a stored procedure to compute the curl of a vector.

5. Write a stored procedure to compute the normal plane, osculating plane and rectifying plane for the TNB frame.

Chapter 6

Statistics

Statistics is where a vast array of procedures exist and can be written using MySQL. This chapter offers only a small fraction of this. I choose popular topics in keeping with the spirit of the text. These topics include examples from the following:

1. Discrete distributions

2. Continuous distributions

3. Random Number Generators

4. Estimation and Hypothesis Tests

5. Bivariate Data

6. Nonparametric Statistics

6.1   Discrete Distributions

Why are we not beginning with the standard measures like mean, median, mode and standard deviation? MySQL already has some of the basic statistical operations available like arithmetic average and standard deviation. Other measures like mode and medians can be done with queries and can often be found on blog pages online. It is also possible to write SP's for these types of calculations if one wishes to consider more general situations such as data sets that are not unimodal or grouped data sets. So rather than take time to discuss these popular calculations we shall show more of what MySQL can do with statistics, beginning with discrete distributions.

The binomial distribution is probably the most popular discrete distribution. It is used as the jumping point for many other discrete distributions as well as acting as an approximation to the normal density. Since this distribution is an important one for the discrete random variables, I have written a stored procedure for the binomial probability density function, or pdf.

```
Delimiter \\
create procedure binomialpdf(
in n int,
in x int,
in p float,
out pdf float)
proc_label: begin
If n < 0 then
select 'Number of trials must be positive.'
       as Error_Message;
leave proc_label;
end if;
If p < 0 or p > 1 then
select 'Probability must be in [0, 1].'
       as Error_Message;
leave proc_label;
end if;
if x > n or x < 0 then
select 'Trial number must be in [0, n].'
       as Error_Message;
leave proc_label;
end if;
If x >= 0 and x <= n then
set @i:= 1;
set @num := 1;
set @den1 := 1;
set @den2 := 1;
While @i <= n do
set @num = @num * @i;
Set @i = @i + 1;
end While;
set @i:= 1;
While @i <= x do
set @den1:= @den1 * @i;
set @i = @i + 1;
end While;
set @i:= 1;
While @i <= n-x do
set @den2 := @den2 * @i;
set @i = @i+1;
end While;
end if;
Select  @num/(@den1 * @den2) * pow(p,x)
```

```
        * pow(1.0 - p, n - x ) into pdf;
set @mean = n*p;
set @stdev = sqrt(n*p(1-p));
end \\
Delimiter ;
```

This particular scheme not only produces specific values for the binomial probability density function, but it also has the mean and standard deviation available
if you wish to have them. These are common measures associated with pdfs.
The Poisson distribution is also a popular discrete distribution. Below is a
stored procedure that computes values for the Poisson pdf.

```
Delimiter \\
create procedure poissonpdf(
in lambda float,
in x int,
out poissonpdf float)
proc_label: begin
set @i = 1;
set @a = 1;
if x < 0 or floor(x) - x <> 0 then
select 'Error: x must be a positive integer' as Error_Message;
leave proc_label;
end if;
while @i <= x do
set @a := @a*@i;
set @i = @i + 1;
end while;
select pow(lambda,x)*exp(-lambda)/@a into poissonpdf;
set @mean = lambda;
set @stdev = sqrt(lambda);
end \\
Delimiter ;
```

There are many other discrete distributions such as the discrete uniform, geometric, hypergeometric and negative binomial to name a few. I encourage you
to research these distributions and generate stored procedures to have a large
portfolio of statistical tools available.

Cumulative distribution functions are the counterpart to probability density
functions. Below we have a cumulative distribution function for the Poisson
density.

```
Delimiter \\
create procedure poissoncdf(
in lambda float,
in x float)
```

```
proc_label: begin
if (floor(x) - x <> 0 or x <=0) then
select 'Error: Random variable value must be a positive integer'
        as Error_Message;
leave proc_label;
end if;
create temporary table poissoncdfvalues(x_value int,
        probability float);
set @j = 0;
while @j <= x do
 set @a = 1;
 set @i = 1;
   while @i <= @j do
   set @a := @a*@i;
   set @i = @i + 1;
   end while;
insert into poissoncdfvalues(x_value, probability)
values (@j, pow(lambda,@j)*exp(-lambda)/@a) ;
set @j = @j + 1;
end while;
set @s = (select sum(probability) from poissoncdfvalues);
set @t = 1- @s;
end \\
Delimiter ;
```

This particular stored procedure has the following available: a table of individual probability values from a Poisson distribution, the cumulative probability (@s) and the complementary probability (@t). This procedure may answer some common questions about a Poisson distribution in a first semester statistics course.

1. Write a stored procedure for the binomial cdf.

2. Write a stored procedure for the geometric pdf and cdf.

3. Write a stored procedure to give information concerning the discrete uniform density. This should include the mean, standard deviation, values on the pdf and values on the cdf.

6.2 Continuous Distributions

Discrete distributions are not the only ones studied in statistics courses and obviously are not the only ones used. Continuous random variables also have their own densities and distributions. The Gaussian, or Normal, density has been studied extensively across the mathematics spectrum as its use spans almost all scientific fields. A stored procedure for a Normal pdf is given below. Notice

there is no error checking or comments in this stored procedure. As an exercise,
I encourage you to fill in these missing pieces.

```
Delimiter \\
create procedure normalpdf(
in x float,
in m float,
in s float)
Begin
set @n = 1.0/sqrt(2*pi()*s) *exp(-pow(x-m,2)/(2.0*pow(s,2)));
end\\
Delimiter ;
```

Below is an algorithm used to construct values for the normal cumulative distribution function. I offer this not only because of the popularity of the Normal cdf, but to demonstrate that many approximation algorithms for non-elementary function do not approximate the integral directly. An approximation to the curve directly is often employed or an iterative solving procedure is used, depending on the complexity of the pdf. This particular algorithm for the Normal cdf has been used as a benchmark for industry strength code as it is at least six digit accurate.

```
Delimiter \\
create procedure normalcdf(
in z float,
out cdf float)
begin
If z > 6.0 then set cdf = 1;
end if;
If z < -6.0 then set cdf = 0;
end if;

/* protects against overflow */

set @b1 = 0.31938153;
set @b2 = -0.356563782;
set @b3 = 1.781477937;
set @b4 = -1.821255978;
set @b5 = 1.330274429;
set @p = 0.2316419;
set @c2 = 0.3989423;
set @a = abs(z)
set @t = 1.0/(1.0 + @a * @p);
set @b = @c2 *exp((-z)*(z/2.0));
set @n = (((((@b5 * @t + @b4)*@t + @b3)*@t + @b2)*@t + @b1)*@t;
set @n = 1.0 - @b * @n;
if z < 0.0 then set @n = 1.0 - @n;
```

```
end if;
select @n into cdf;
end \\
Delimiter ;
```

There are quite a large number of cumulative distribution functions, many of which require numerical techniques for evaluations. I encourage you to research these schemes and code stored procedures for these cdfs especially if you plan on pursuing statistics with SQL or MySQL. For additional practice to whet your appetite, I offer the following exercises which have much less complicated mathematical descriptions.

1. Write a stored procedure for the cdf for the exponential distribution.

2. Write a stored procedure for the cdf for the Weibull distribution.

3. For the ambitious: Write stored procedures for the Student T distribution and Fischer's F distribution.

6.3   Random Number Generators

Random numbers are a common tool used in statistical simulations and no discussion using programming and statistics would be complete without it. Below I present a stored procedure for generating n random values with a Normal density. This particular method is known as the Polar Marsaglia Method and is common in industry.

```
Delimiter \\
create procedure Normal_Random_Number(
in n int)
begin
create temporary table normrv(a int, b float);
set @i = 1;
while @i <= n do
set @S = 2;
while @S>=1 do
set @a = rand();
set @b = rand();
set @v = 2*@a - 1.0;
set @w = 2*@b - 1.0;
set @S = pow(@v,2) + pow(@w,2);
end while;
Set @X = @v*sqrt((-2.0*log(@S))/@S);
insert into normrv
values(@i, @X);
set @i = @i + 1;
end while;
```

```
end\\
Delimiter ;
```

This stored procedure uses the command **rand()** and as you probably guessed, this is MySQL's random number generator. This command will generate a uniformly distributed random value in the interval $(0, 1)$. This particular code has been used in many other programming languages, including C. Many other psuedo-random number generators may be programmed in MySQL and I encourage mimicry using another language like C which are readily available.

1. Write a stored procedure to generate n random numbers which have a geometric distribution.

2. Write a stored procedure to generate n random numbers which have a χ^2-distribution.

3. Create a random number generator that will generate integer values only, to simulate the toss of a die. You may wish to add the ability to choose a fair or unfair die as is common in practice. Six sides is also not necessary. There exists die that have 2 (a coin), 4, 8, 10, 12, 20 and 100 to name a few non-standard dice.

6.4   Estimation and Hypothesis Tests

Estimation of parameters, also known as confidence intervals, are an essential part of statistical analysis. Using technology to estimate these is commonplace. Below is an algorithm for generating a confidence interval for the mean when the population standard deviation is known.

```
Delimiter \\
create procedure ZInterval(
in est float,
in stdev float,
in clevel float,
in samplesize int)
proc_label: Begin
if (samplesize - floor(samplesize)<> 0 or samplesize < 1) then
select 'Error: Sample size must be an integer at least 1'
      as Error_Message;
leave proc_label;
end if;
if stdev <= 0 then
select 'Error: standard deviation must be a positive value'
      as Error_Message;
leave proc_label;
end if;
if (clevel >= 1 or clevel <= 0) then
```

```
select 'Error: Confidence level must be a value in (0,1)'
       as Error_Message;
leave proc_label;
end if;
set @p = (1.0 - clevel)/2.0;
set @Y=SQRT(-2.0*LOG(@p));
set @z=@Y-(((((4.53642210148*pow(10,-5)*@Y +
       2.04231210245*pow(10,-2))*@Y +
     3.42242088547*pow(10,-1))*@Y+1)*@Y +
              .322232431088)
 /(((((3.8560700634*pow(10,-3)*@Y +
       1.0353775285*pow(10,-1))*@Y +
            5.31103462366*pow(10,-1))*@Y +
              5.88581570495*pow(10,-1))*@Y
                  +.099348462606);
set @lower = est - @z*stdev/sqrt(samplesize);
set @upper = est + @z*stdev/sqrt(samplesize);
end\\
Delimiter ;
```

Other confidence intervals may also be generated as long as an accurate inverse cumulative distribution function can be used. These functions are often difficult to approximate and are a current research topic in numerical analysis and computational statistics. If you wish to investigate such intervals for generating these confidence intervals I definitely encourage it. The Student T, the Chi-Square and F-distributions are the most popular and have many simple approximations under certain conditions. The exponential and Weibull distributions are also popular ones which have simpler mathematical descriptions. These two may be a good starting place for increasing your experience.

Hypothesis testing is also another integral component of statistical analysis. There are plenty of procedures to choose from that are implemented in courses. Below is probably the most popular test in introductory statistics courses, the Z-Test.

```
Delimiter \\
create procedure ZTest(
in popmean float,
in popstdev float,
in sampmean float,
in n int,
in siglevel float,
in testtype int,
out zscore float,
out pvalue float,
out decision varchar(30))
proc_label: begin
```

```
/* Error checking to make sure correct values
 are input into testing procedure. Adjustments
are made for most cases of erroneous inputs.*/

if siglevel <= 0.0 or siglevel >= 1.0 then
select 'Error: Significance level must be in (0,1)';
leave proc_label;
end if;
If popstdev <=0 then
select 'Error: Population Standard Deviation must be positive';
leave proc_label;
end if;
if testtype < 0 then set testtype = -1;
end if;
if testtype > 0 then set testtype = 1;
end if;
if ceil(n) - n <> 0 then set n = floor(n);
end if;
if n <=0   then
select 'Error: Sample Size must be a positive integer';
leave proc_label;
end if;
set @x := (sampmean - popmean)/(popstdev/sqrt(n));
If @x > 6.0 then
   set pvalue = 1;
end if;
If @x < -6.0 then
   set pvalue = 0;
end if;

 /* protects against overflow */

If abs(@x) <= 6.0 then
set @b1 = 0.31938153;
set @b2 = -0.356563782;
set @b3 = 1.781477937;
set @b4 = -1.821255978;
set @b5 = 1.330274429;
set @p = 0.2316419;
set @c2 = 1.0/sqrt(2.0*pi());
set @a = abs(@x);
set @t = 1.0/(1.0 + @a * @p);
set @b = @c2 *exp((-@x)*(@x/2.0));
set @n = (((((@b5 * @t + @b4)*@t + @b3)*@t + @b2)*@t + @b1)*@t;
set @y = 1.0 - @b * @n;
```

```
select @x into zscore;
case testtype when -1
   then select @y into pvalue;
when 1
   then select 1.0 - @y into pvalue;
else
    select least(@y, 1.0 - @y)*2.0 into pvalue;
end case;
if pvalue <= siglevel then
select 'Reject Null Hypothesis' into decision;
else
select 'Fail to Reject Null Hypothesis' into decision;
end if;
end if;
end\\
Delimiter ;
```

This procedure has the normalcdf reproduced so it may run independently. If
you already have a stored procedure for the Normal cdf, see if you can call the
stored procedure inside this one. The syntax for the call function does not need
to be changed. Be aware of the label for the output so you may use it here
appropriately.

Our last example of using MySQL with hypothesis tests and estimation is a
Goodness of Fit test with the uniform distribution.

```
Delimiter \\
create procedure UnifGOF()
proc_label: Begin
create temporary table observeGOF(obsnumber int, observed float);
insert into observeGOF(obsnumber, observed)
values(1, 27),(2,31),(3,42),(4,40),(5,28),(6,32);
set @expected = (select sum(observed)/count(observed)
      from observeGOF);
set @score = (select sum(pow(observed - @expected,2)/@expected)
      from observeGOF);
set @m = (select count(observed) from observeGOF);
set @k = @m - 1;

/*Approximation of chi-sqsuare distribution,
We approximate the numerator, lower incomplete
Gamma function with Gaussian Quadrature.
This integrand needed a change of variable in
order to make it work correctly.*/

create temporary table LegendreX(Zcounter int,
    legendre_zero float);
```

```
insert into LegendreX(Zcounter, Legendre_zero)
values(1, -0.906179845938664),
(2,-0.538469310105683),
(3, 0.0),
(4,0.538469310105683),
(5,0.906179845938664);

create temporary table GaussW(Wcounter int, weighting float);
insert into GaussW(Wcounter, weighting)
values(1, 0.236926885056189),
(2, 0.478628670499366),
(3,0.568888888888889),
(4,0.478628670499366),
(5,0.236926885056189);

/*function x^(k/2-1) e^(-x)) is the integrand
 and is hard-coded as function to integrate from -1 to 1.
 We needed to make a transformation to make this
 happen. */

create temporary table QuadVals(integral_values float);
set @j = 1;
while @j <= 5 do
insert into QuadVals(integral_values)
 (select  0.25*@score * a.weighting*pow((@score*b.legendre_zero
      + @score)*0.25,@k/2.0 - 1.0)*
 exp(-1.0*(@score * b.legendre_zero+@score)*0.25) from GaussW a
join LegendreX b on a.Wcounter = b.Zcounter
where a.Wcounter = @j and b.Zcounter = @j);
set @j = @j + 1;
end while;
set @lowergamma = (select sum(integral_values) from QuadVals);

/*Gamma(k/2) is a factor in the denominator
for the chi-square cdf. */

if (@k < 0 or floor(@k) - @k <> 0) then
select 'Error: input must be a positive integer' as Error_Message;
leave proc_label;
end if;
set @i = 1;
set @g = 1;
if (floor(@k/2) - @k/2 = 0) then
while @i <=(@k/2.0 - 1) do
set @g = @g * @i;
set @i = @i + 1;
```

```
end while;
else
set @num = 1;
set @denom = 1;
set @n = (@k-1)/2.0;
while @i <= @n do
set @num = @num * @i;
set @denom = @denom*@i;
set @i = @i + 1;
end while;
while @i <= 2*@n do
set @num = @num *@i;
set @i = @i + 1;
end while;
set @g = @num*sqrt(pi())/(pow(4,@n)*@denom);
end if;
set @p = @lowergamma/@g;
end\\
Delimiter ;
call UnifGOF();
select @score as teststat, 1-@p as pvalue;
```

I included the select statement because the @p variable represents the area under the curve. We are interested in the area that is left over as the definition of P-value suggests.

This code is a hodgepodge of three codes: the first one being the computation of the expected values, the second being the computation of the lower Gamma function via Gaussian Quadrature with five nodes and the third being the computation of the gamma function with the argument cut in half. Each one of these would make decent functions on their own and most people would encourage that so they may be used again, with modifications made as needed. I put them together so codes may stand alone. When dealing with a programming language like SQL or MySQL, breaking things apart is definitely more desirable. This particular stored procedure, I think, demonstrates why the "less is more" approach is used.

With reliable approximations of cdf functions, other hypothesis tests may be generated. Again, I encourage you to pursue this. The T-Test, Chi-Square tests and the F-Test are among a few popular tests where a plethora of approximations to cdfs exists and may be easily obtained.

6.5 Bivariate Data

Before we get to any more stored procedures, we need to discuss a very important reality. More often than not, lists of data are available for analysis and not statistical measures directly. This implies we need to have the ability to bring lists into stored procedures. An unfoturnate thing is this happens to an area where SQL and MySQL differ. With SQL, using a declare statement and an execute command is usually enough to accomplish this task. MySQL, on the other hand, does not operate this way. There is a lot more to bringing in lists and tables into a stored procedure. At this time, this concept is not an easy one. With that being said, these next few demonstrations will be queries and not procedures.

Since statistics is not a univariate study, it seems natural to begin examining processes using bivariate data. This brings to mind the covariance, the Pearson correlation coefficient and of course, linear least-squares regression. Covariance is probably the first calculation involving bivariate data that is performed in statistics courses. That being the case, I show one such query first. There are others available online. I first create tables in order to use my query.

```
create table Xvalues(dataval int, x float);
insert into Xvalues(dataval, x)
values(1,1),(2,2),(3,3),(4,4),(5,5);
create table Yvalues(dataval int, y float);
insert into Yvalues (dataval, y)
values(1,5),(2,7),(3,10),(4,15),(5,24);
set @averagex = (select avg(x) from Xvalues);
set @averagey=(select avg(y)  from Yvalues);
set @n = (select count(x)  from Xvalues);
select (1/(@n-1))*sum((x - @averagex)*(y - @averagey))
       as covariance  from xvalues
join yvalues on xvalues.dataval = yvalues.dataval;
```

I kept my data lists short here so I did not use the auto_increment command. It is a good practice in MySQL to get in the habit of establishing a primary key. If your data lists are long, you may also wish to invoke an auto_increment command so you may automatically number the rows. This helps with joining tables together since these would be unique identifiers.

This query use the **join** command again. I did not put the data into one table and compute the covariance because I want to keep these data values separate in case I need to modify some information in one list only. Most books on SQL and MySQL have chapters dedicated to the join command, so we will not repeat that information here. Feel free to use your own tables to compute covariance using this query. By the way, is the calculation for samples or populations? How do you know?

Pearson's correlation coefficient is directly related to covariance. In fact, the covariance is the numerator of the fraction that makes up the correlation. The product of the standard deviations is the denominator. Using the same tables created for the covariance query, we have a query for determining Pearson's correlation coefficient.

```
set @averagex = (select avg(x) from Xvalues);
set @averagey=(select avg(y)  from Yvalues);
set @n = (select count(x)  from Xvalues);
set @cov = (select (1/(@n-1))*sum((x - @averagex)*(y - @averagey))
     from xvalues
join yvalues on xvalues.dataval = yvalues.dataval);
set @sx = (select stddev_samp(x) from xvalues);
set @sy = (select stddev_samp(y) from yvalues);
set @correlation = @cov/(@sx * @sy);
select @correlation;
```

Rather than manipulate the correlation to fit our needs for the least-squares regression line, I shall mimic formulas often found in texts. The reason for this is to stay consistent with what students typically see. Again, using the same tables as before, a query for linear regression is offered below.

```
set @n = (select count(x) from Xvalues);
set @sumx = (select sum(x) from Xvalues);
set @sumy = (select sum(y) from Yvalues);
set @sumxy = (select sum(xvalues.x * yvalues.y) from Xvalues
join Yvalues on xvalues.dataval = Yvalues.dataval);
set @sumxx = (select (sum(pow(x,2))) from Xvalues);
set @sumx2 = pow(@sumx,2);
set @b0 = (@n *@sumxy - @sumx * @sumy)/(@n *@sumxx - @sumx2);
set @b1 = (select avg(y) - @b0* avg(x) from Xvalues
join Yvalues on xvalues.dataval = yvalues.dataval);
select @b0 as slope, @b1 as y_intercept;
```

The advantage of approaching linear regression this way is you have access to all values that are computed for each of the components, the slope and *y*-intercept. This procedure can be altered to produce the results in a table format for easy reading. Try it.

6.6 Nonparametric Statistics

Nonparametric statistics, or distribution-free methods, form an important part of statistical analysis. They also form a useful application of MySQL procedures. The runs test for randomness and the signs test are two such tests that can be used. Stored procedures for these are shown below. We first show a stored procedure for the runs test for randomness that is introduced in an introductory course.

```
Delimiter \\
create procedure runstest(
```

```
in G int,
in n1 int,
in n2 int,
in siglevel float,
out zscore float)
proc_label: Begin
set @muG = NULL;
set @varG = NULL;
if (G < 0 or floor(G) - G <> 0) then
select 'Number of runs must be a positive integer'
    as Error_Message;
leave proc_label;
end if;
if G > n1 + n2 then
select 'Number of runs cannot exceed sum of successes for
        both variables' as Error_Message;
leave proc_label;
end if;
if (n1 < 0 or floor(n1) - n1 <> 0) then
select 'Number of successes for variable 1 must be a
        positive integer' as Error_Message;
leave proc_label;
end if;
if (n2 < 0 or floor(n2) - n2 <> 0) then
select 'Number of successes for variable 2 must be a
        positive integer' as Error_Message;
leave proc_label;
end if;
if (n1 > 20 and siglevel <> 0.05) or
        (n2 > 20 and siglevel <> 0.05) then
set @muG = (2.0*n1*n2)/(n1 + n2) + 1.0;
set @varG = sqrt((((@muG-1)*(@muG - 2))/(n1+ n2 - 1));
set @z = (G - @muG)/@varG;
else
set @z = G;
end if;
set @run = G;
select @z into zscore;
end \\
Delimiter ;
```

The signs test is used to test claims about the median of a distribution. A stored procedure for the signs test is shown below.

```
Delimiter \\
create procedure signstest(
```

```
in x int,
in y int)
/* The input is the number of successes, x
and the number of failures y.
*/
proc_label: Begin
if (x < 0 or floor(x) - x <> 0) then
select 'The number of times a sign occurs must be a
    positive integer' as Error_Message;
leave proc_label;
end if;
if (y <= 0 or floor(y) - y <> 0) then
select 'The number of times a sign occurs must be a
    positive integer' as Error_Message;
leave proc_label;
end if;
set @n = x + y;
set @m = least(x,y);
if @n <= 25 then
set @z = @m;
else
set @z = (@m + 0.5 - @n/2.0)/(sqrt(@n) / 2.0);
end if;
end \\
Delimiter ;
```

Many nonparametric statistics are based on ranks. MySQL differs from SQL in that it does not have a rank function already available. This implies we would have to code one ourselves. There are a few queries online where one may find a rank function for MySQL. My favorite is found at:

http://stackoverflow.com/questions/24118393/mysql-rank-with-ties

and is authored by Aziz Shaikh. If you believe you are going to use ranks often, you may want to save a rank function as a separate function or procedure in your database so you may call it as needed.

One such nonparametric test that uses ranks directly is Spearman's Rank Correlation Coefficient. I offer the following query. This particular query does not use a rank function. I implore you to add a rank function query to this to avoid some unnecessary calculations. Also note this procedure is self-contained, but if you have programmed an inverse cdf function for the normal density (Spearman's rank test uses it if the sample size is greater than 30), you may call this function or stored procedure rather than copying it here. I encourage this, again following the 'less is more' approach.

```
/* This procedure is to be used
```

```
once the data is ranked. I am
entering two lists of ranked data
It is written as a procedure so
there will not be errors when
calling if-statements, etc.*/

Delimiter \\
create procedure SpearmansRank()
proc_label:Begin

/*original data lists just in case ranks are tied*/

create temporary table origdata1(dataposorig1 int,
      origval1 float);
insert into origdata1(dataposorig1, origval1)
values (1,4),(2,2),(3,5),(4,1),(5,3),(6,6),(7,7),(8,8),
   (9,9), (10,9);

create temporary table origdata2(dataposorig2 int,
       origval2 float);
insert into origdata2(dataposorig2, origval2)
values (1,2),(2,6),(3,7),(4,3),(5,1),(6,10),(7,4),(8,8),
   (9,5), (10,9);

/*ranked data lists, a ranking query may be
used here to take care of these extra tables
*/

create temporary table rankeddata1(datapos1 int,
       rankvalue1 float);
insert into rankeddata1(datapos1, rankvalue1)
values (1,4),(2,2),(3,5),(4,1),(5,3),(6,6),(7,7),(8,8),
   (9,9), (10,9);

create temporary table rankeddata2(datapos2 int,
       rankvalue2 float);
insert into rankeddata2(datapos2, rankvalue2)
values (1,2),(2,6),(3,7),(4,3),(5,1),(6,10),(7,4),(8,8),
   (9,5), (10,9);

set @n = (select count(rankvalue1) from rankeddata1);
set @m = (select count(rankvalue2) from rankeddata2);

if @m <> @n then
Select 'Dimension mismatch, data lists must have
the same number of values' as Error_Message;
```

```
leave proc_label;
end if;

/* Formulas are different if ties occur */

if ((select sum(rankvalue1) = @n*(@n+1)/2.0 from rankeddata1) and
        (select sum(rankvalue2) = @m*(@m+1)/2.0
        from rankeddata2)) then
set @r = (select sum(pow(a.rankvalue1 - b.rankvalue2,2))
        from rankeddata1 a join rankeddata2 b
        on a.datapos1 = b.datapos2);
set @r = 1-6*@r/(@n*(pow(@n,2)-1));
else
set @r = (select (@n*sum(c.origval1 * d.origval2) -
    sum(c.origval1)*sum(d.origval2))/(sqrt(@n *
    sum(pow(c.origval1,2)) - pow(sum(c.origval1),2)) *
    sqrt(@n * sum(pow(d.origval2,2)) - pow(sum(d.origval2),2)))
    from origdata1 c join origdata2 d
    on c.dataposorig1 = d.dataposorig2);
end if;

if @n <= 30 then
Select 'Use Tables to find critical values'
      as Message;
else
set @clevel = 0.95;
set @p = (1.0 - @clevel)/2.0;
set @Y=SQRT(-2.0*LOG(@p));
set @z=@Y-((((4.53642210148*pow(10,-5)*@Y
+2.04231210245*pow(10,-2))*@Y
+3.42242088547*pow(10,-1))*@Y+1)*@Y
+.322232431088)
 /((((3.8560700634*pow(10,-3)*@Y
 +1.0353775285*pow(10,-1))*@Y
 +5.31103462366*pow(10,-1))*@Y
 +5.88581570495*pow(10,-1))*@Y
 +.099348462606);
set @rcv = abs(@z/sqrt(@n - 1));
end if;
end\\
Delimiter ;
```

Chapter 7

Differential Equations

In this chapter we explore introductory methods for solving differential equations. Since many differential equations require numerical methods to solve them, I believe it would be an injustice not to demonstrate two popular solving methods for ordinary differential equations. Solving differential equations using numerical methods is a well established field in applied mathematics and there are many texts devoted to the subject. We list our topics here.

1. Euler's Method

2. Runge-Kutta Method (RK4)

3. Finite Difference Scheme for the Heat Equation

4. Bessel Functions

7.1   Euler's Method

Euler's Method is typically the first numerical scheme demonstrated in a differential equations course. This scheme is not strong and is usually not used in industry as there are much, much stronger schemes. Keeping in the spirit of this text though it will suit our purposes.

```
Delimiter \\
create procedure EulerMethod(
in leftend float,
in rightend float,
in N int,
in initcon float)
Begin

/*Setting up initial values for loop */
```

```
Set @h = (rightend - leftend)/N;
Set @t = leftend;
Set @w = initcon;
Set @i = 1;
create temporary table EulerTable( i float, approx float);
insert into EulerTable(i,approx)
values (@t, @w);

/* f(t,y) = -y + t + 1 is hard-coded into the loop.
Change this for other functions */

while @i <= N do
set @w = @w + @h * (-@w + @t + 1.0); /* <--- f(t,y) is here in () */
set @t = leftend + @i*@h;
set @i = @i+1;
insert into EulerTable(i,approx)
values (@t, @w);
end while;
end\\
Delimiter ;
```

1. While there are stronger schemes in industry there are improvements that can be made to the Euler Method. The Improved Euler Method is given below.

$$y_{i+1} = y_i + \frac{h}{2} \left[f(t_i, y_i) + f(t_{i+1}, y_{i+1} + hf(t_i, y_i)) \right]$$

for $i = 1, 2, \ldots, N$. See if you can add this stored procedure to your portfolio.

2. Heun's method is another improvement over the Euler method.

$$y_0 = a_0$$

$$y_{i+1} = y_i + \frac{h}{4} \left(f(t_i, y_i) + 3f(t_i + \frac{2}{3}h, w_i + \frac{2}{3}hf(t_i, y_i)) \right)$$

for $i = 1, 2, \ldots, N$. Add this stored procedure to your portfolio.

7.2   Runge-Kutta Method (RK4)

One of the more popular schemes for differential equations is the Fourth-Order Runge-Kutta Method or RK4. Here we have the RK4 Method as well.

```
Delimiter \\
create procedure RK4(
in leftend float,
```

```
in rightend float,
in N int,
in initcon float)
Begin

/* Initial values for local variables */

Set @h = (rightend - leftend)/N;
Set @t = leftend;
Set @w = initcon;
Set @i = 1;

/* Creating table to store approximate values */

create temporary table RKTable(t float, approx float);
insert into RKTable(t, approx)
values (@t, @w);

/* f(t,y) = -y + t + 1 is hard-coded into the loop
for each of the @K_i values */

while @i <= N do
Set @K1 = @h *(-@w + @t + 1.0);
Set @K2 = @h * (-(@w + @K1/2.0) + @t + @h/2.0 + 1);
Set @K3 = @h * (-(@w + @K2/2.0) + @t + @h/2.0 + 1);
Set @K4 = @h * (-(@w + @K3) + @t + @h + 1);
Set @w = @w + (@K1 + 2.0*@K2 + 2.0 * @K3 + @k4)/6.0;
Set @t = leftend + @i * @h;
Set @i = @i + 1;
insert into RKTable(t, approx)
values(@t, @w);
end while;
end \\
Delimiter ;
```

The RK4 Method can even be extended to a scheme called the Runge-Kutta-Fehlberg method and it can even be extended to systems of differential equations. If you are interested in this topic, research these schemes and try to write a procedure. For continued practice though we will explore predictor-corrector methods.

1. There are an assortment of predictor-corrector methods as well. One of the simplest predictor-corrector methods is the Adams-Bashforth Two-Step Method.

$$y_0 = a_0$$

$$y_1 = a_1$$

$$y_{i+1} = y_i + \frac{h}{2}\left(3f(t_i, y_i) - f(t_{i-1}, y_{i-1})\right)$$

for $i = 1, 2, \ldots, N - 1$.

2. We've seen explicit schemes so far, but there are implicit schemes as well. Below is an implicit predictor-corrector method known as the fourth-order Adams-Moulton technique.

$$y_0 = a_0$$

$$y_1 = a_1$$

$$y_2 = a_2$$

$$y_{i+1} = y_i + \frac{h}{24}\left[9f(t_{i+1}, y_{i+1}) + 19f(t_i, y_i) - 5f(t_{i-1}, y_{i-1}) + f(t_{i-2}, y_{i-2})\right]$$

for $i = 1, 2, \ldots, N$.

7.3 Finite Difference Scheme for the Heat Equation

The heat equation, or the diffusion equation, is often the first parabolic partial differential equation studied. Some popular equations, such as the Black-Scholes Equation from finance, can be rewritten through variable transformations as the heat equation. In this particular section, I demonstrate a stored procedure for an explicit scheme for determining the solution to the one-dimensional heat equation with the boundary conditions equal to zero at the ends (in this case $0 < x < 1$) and the initial condition is $u(x, 0) = sin(\pi x)$. We only consider ten steps in both the time direction and the spatial direction.

```
Delimiter \\
create procedure ExplicitFDHeat(
in diffconst float,
in rightend float,
in maxtime float,
in m int,
in n int)

/*n is the number of time steps and
m is the number of spatial steps*/

Begin
set @h = rightend/m;
set @k = maxtime/n;
```

```
set @lambda = diffconst*@k/pow(@h,2);
set @i = 1;
set @j = 1;

/*@i is the counter for the spatial
movement, @j is the counter for
the temporal movement*/

create temporary table approxsoln(timecounter int, spacecounter int,
      timestep float, spacestep float, fncvalue float);

/*initial condition entering into table*/

insert into approxsoln(timecounter, spacecounter, timestep,
      spacestep, fncvalue)
values(0, 0, 0, 0, 0);
while @i <= m - 1 do
insert into approxsoln(timecounter, spacecounter, timestep,
      spacestep, fncvalue)
values (0,@i,0, @i*@h, sin(pi() * @i * @h));
set @i = @i + 1;
end while;
insert into approxsoln(timecounter, spacecounter, timestep,
      spacestep,fncvalue)
values(0, m, 0, rightend, 0);
while @j <= n do
   insert into approxsoln(timecounter, spacecounter, timestep,
      spacestep, fncvalue)
   values(@j, 0, @j*@k, 0, 0);
   set @i = 1;
      while @i <= m - 1 do
        set @foldback = (select fncvalue from approxsoln
        where timecounter = @j - 1 and spacecounter = @i - 1);
        set @foldmiddle = (select fncvalue from approxsoln
        where timecounter = @j - 1 and spacecounter = @i);
        set @foldforward = (select fncvalue from approxsoln
        where timecounter = @j - 1 and spacecounter = @i + 1);
        insert into approxsoln(timecounter, spacecounter, timestep,
            spacestep, fncvalue)
        values(@j, @i, @j*@h, @i*@k,
        @foldback*@lambda + (1-2*@lambda)*@foldmiddle +
            @lambda * @foldforward);
        set @i = @i + 1;
   end while;
   insert into approxsoln(timecounter, spacecounter, timestep,
            spacestep, fncvalue)
```

```
    values (@j, m, @j*@h, rightend, 0);
    set @j = @j + 1;
end while;
end\\
Delimiter ;
```

One major concern with explicit schemes is their stability. It is known that in order for this particular scheme to be stable, our variable @lambda must be strictly less than 0.5. If you execute this procedure with the following command: *call ExplicitFDHeat(1,1,1,10,10)*, you may see unreasonable behavior as shown in Figure 1 and Figure 2 at the end of this chapter. This is because the stability criteria is violated (@lambda = 10 in this case). See Figures 3 and 4 at the end of this chapter at the end of this chapter to see results when the stability criteria is satisfied (@lambda = 0.001). These images were generated from Excel by simply copying and pasting the results of the procedure into Excel and then choosing the Scatter Plot option.

1. Consider the one-dimensional wave equation. Write a stored procedure for an explicit finite difference scheme to determine the solution values to this equation.

2. Consider Laplace's equation. Write a stored procedure for an explicit finite difference scheme to determine the solution values to this equation.

7.4   Bessel Functions

Our last section of this unit investigates the Bessel functions. Bessel functions are members of a larger class of functions, known as the Special Functions. These functions are usually solutions to special types of differential equations and are a topic of study in mathematics. Bessel functions are chosen here as an example of a common question, "What's the best way to handle this situation?" The answer is commonly, "What are you trying to do?" There are many ways to represent Bessel functions. One popular way is through the series:

$$J_v(x) = \sum_{n=0}^{\infty} \frac{(-1)^n}{n!\Gamma(1+v+n)} \left(\frac{x}{2}\right)^{2n+v}$$

and another way is through an integral:

$$J_v(x) = \frac{1}{\pi} \int_0^\pi \cos(x\sin\theta - v\theta)d\theta$$

Suppose our task is to generate points for a Bessel function of zero order for plotting. We then need an approximation to the coefficients of x at given values of x. Below is a stored procedures for the series approach. Plots of using the first five terms and the first seven terms are shown and compared with Excel (Excel has a BesselJ function in their Function $\rightarrow$ Engineering menu.) I ask you to try to improve upon the results either by

a. Adding more terms to the series, or

b. A numerical integration technique, or

c. A polynomial approximation that you may research, or even

d. A different type of series representation.

```
Delimiter \\
create procedure BesselJSeries(
in n float)
Begin
set @i = 1;
create temporary table Bessel(xvalcount int, inputx float,
      outputy float);
create temporary table Num(xvalcounter int, xcoords float,
      numerator float);
while @i <= 40 do
create temporary table Factbot(counter int, factvals int);
set @j = 1;
set @fact = 1;
while @j <= n do
set @fact = @fact*@j;
insert into Factbot(counter, factvals)
values(@j, pow(@fact,2));
set @num = pow(-1,@j)*0.25*pow(pow(@i/10,2),@j);
insert into Num(xvalcounter, xcoords, numerator)
values(@j,@i/10, @num);
set @j = @j + 1;
end while;
set @b = (select sum(a.numerator / b.factvals) from Num a
join Factbot b on a.xvalcounter = b.counter);
set @b = @b + 1;
insert into Bessel(xvalcount, inputx, outputy)
values(@i, @i/10, @b);
drop temporary table Factbot;
set @i = @i+1;
end while;
end\\
Delimiter ;
\end\\
```

Figure 5 at the end of this chapter shows the results of applying this scheme with five terms in the series and seven terms in the series. The fact that Excel has a much better approximation to the Bessel functions suggests better techniques are available.

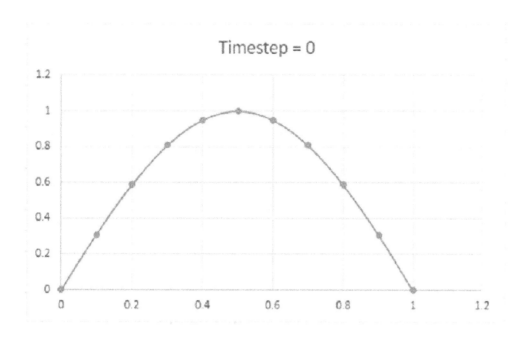

Figure 7.1: Example of Unstable Evaluation $t = 0$.

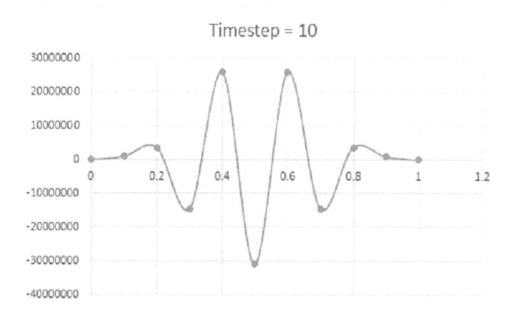

Figure 7.2: Example of Unstable Evaluation, $t = 10$.

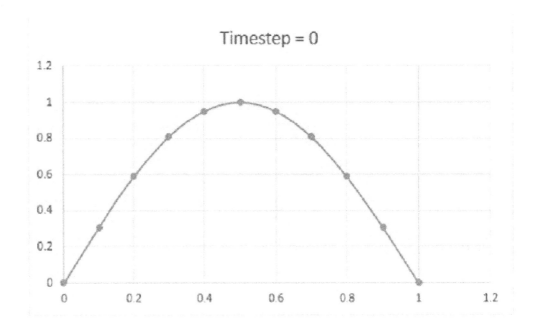

Figure 7.3: Example of Stable Evaluation, t = 0.

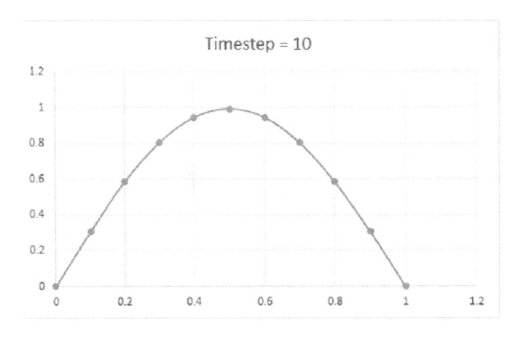

Figure 7.4: Example of Stable Evaluation, t = 10.

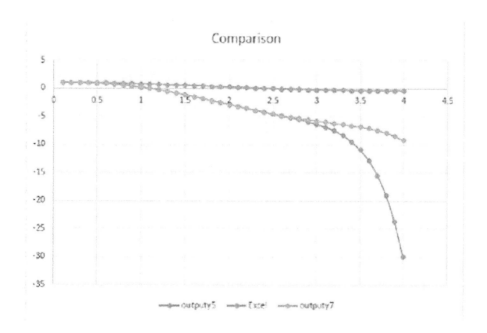

Figure 7.5: Series Approximation to $J_0(x)$.

Chapter 8

Other SPs For Mathematics

In this final chapter, I select three other ideas to code in as queries or stored procedures. These are more or less personal choices based on my interests or concepts researched during my employment.

1. Some Combinatorics Results

2. Minisum Method

3. Euler-Maruyama Method

8.1 Some Combinatorics Results

Counting rules are especially popular in statistics, probability, discrete mathematics and contemporary mathematics but have found roots in combinatorics. These are often programmed on modern day calculators as well. Permutations and combinations are probably the most common counting formulas for determining the number of ways objects may be selected from a group. The following stored procedure is for both the combination $_nC_r$ and permutation $_nP_r$ since they are very closely related mathematically.

```
Delimiter \\
create procedure CountingRules(
in n int,
in x int,
out C varchar(255),
out P varchar(255))
Begin
If n < x then
Select 0 into C;
Select 0 into P;
end if;
If n < 0 then
```

```
Select 'NULL' into C;
Select 'NULL' into P;
end if;
If x < 0 then
Select 'NULL' into C;
Select 'NULL' into P;
end if;
If n = 0 and x = 0 then
Select 1 into C;
Select 1 into P;
end If;
If n = 0 and x <> 0 then
Select 0 into C;
Select 0 into P;
end If;
If x > 0 and x <= n then
set @i:= 1;
set @num := 1;
set @den1 := 1;
set @den2 := 1;
set @num2 := 1;
set @den3 := 1;
While @i <= n do
set @num = @num * @i;
Set @i = @i+1;
end While;
set @i:= 1;
While @i <= x do
set @den1:= @den1 * @i;
set @i = @i+1;
end While;
Set @i:= 1;
While @i <= n-x do
set @den2 := @den2 * @i;
set @i = @i+1;
end While;
Select @num/(@den1 * @den2) into C;
Select @num/@den2 into P;
end if;
end \\
Delimiter ;
```

The permutation is used to compute the number of ways objects may be selected when order matters. Combinations are used when order does not matter. These rules are used when replacement is not permitted. See if you can answer the following questions.

1. Write a stored procedure for the distinguishable permutations.

2. Write a stored procedure to determine the number of ways of selecting objects from a group where replacement is permitted and order does not matter. The formula for such a calculation is given below. Here n is the number of objects to select from and r is the number of objects we are selecting with replacement allowed.

$$\frac{(n+r-1)!}{(n-1)!r!}$$

Another result that is common in combinatorics is the double factorial, $n!!$. This does not mean to apply the factorial operation twice, it is defined as follows:

$$n!! = \begin{cases} n(n-2)(n-4)\cdots(3)(1) & \text{if } n \text{ is odd} \\ n(n-2)(n-4)\cdots(4)(2) & \text{if } n \text{ is even} \\ 1 & \text{if } n = -1, 0 \end{cases}$$

This particular procedure does not entertain the inputs of zero or negative one, add in comments and any error messages or outputs that may be needed.

```
Delimiter \\
create procedure Double_Factorial(
in n int,
out semifactorial int)
begin
set @k := 0;
set @x := 1.0;
set @m := ceil(n/2) - 1;
While (@k <= @m) do
set @x := @x * (n - 2*@k);
set @k := @k + 1;
end while;
select @x into semifactorial;
end\\
Delimiter ;
```

It is not feasible to discuss factorials without mentioning the Gamma function,

$$\Gamma(x) = \int_0^\infty x^{t-1}e^{-x}dx$$

In the statistics chapter with the chi-square goodness of fit example, we saw a section of the stored procedure that evaluated $\Gamma(k/2)$ where k was a positive integer. The full Gamma function with an arbitrary input has many approximations. You might be considering using a Gaussian Quadrature method, similar to the one done for the goodness of fit example, but the infinty in the upper limit of the integral suggests an approximating function may be better. There are many papers and websites dedicated to approximating this important function.

8.2 Minisum Method

The field that closely intersects mathematics with business operations is Operations Research. Many problems associated with business are studied mathematically in this field. One major question that often needs answering is facility location. Below is a query from Operations Research used in facility location, known as the Minisum Method.

```
create table minisumdata (suppliernumber int, xcoord int,
     ycoord int, weight int);
insert into minisumdata
(suppliernumber, xcoord, ycoord, weight)
values(1,1,1,5),
(2,5,2,6),
(3,2,8,2),
(4,4,4,4),
(5,8,6,8);

/* finding cut-off based on median */

set @cutoff := (select sum(weight)/2 from minisumdata);
select @cutoff;

/* sorting table and running total for x coordinate */

create temporary table sortx
select a.suppliernumber, a.xcoord, a.ycoord, a.weight
from minisumdata a
order by xcoord;
SET @runtot=0;
create temporary table runningtotal
Select q1.d,
q1.x,
q1.c,
(@runtot := @runtot + q1.c)
as rt
from
   (select suppliernumber as d, xcoord as x,
 weight as c
from  sortx
    where  suppliernumber > 0
group by d
    order by xcoord) AS q1
where @runtot < @cutoff;

/* sorting table and running total for y coordinate */
```

```
create temporary table sorty
select a.suppliernumber, a.xcoord, a.ycoord, a.weight
from minisumdata a
order by ycoord;
set @runtot=0;
create temporary table runningtotal2
Select q1.d,
q1.y,
q1.c,
(@runtot := @runtot + q1.c) as rt
from
    (select
        suppliernumber as d,
        ycoord as y,
        weight as c
from  sorty
where  suppliernumber > 0
group  by d
order  by ycoord) AS q1
where @runtot < @cutoff;
/* Coordinates for optimal location via minisum method */

/* x coordinate */

set @XX := (select x from runningtotal
where rt > @cutoff order by rt desc limit 1);

/* y coordinate */

set @YY := (select y from runningtotal2 b
where rt > @cutoff order by rt desc limit 1);

/*objective function value based on Rectangular metric */

set @OBJ:= (select sum(weight *(abs(xcoord - @XX) +
      abs(ycoord - @YY))) from minisumdata);

/* objective function value based on Euclidean metric */

set @OBJ2 := (select
sum(weight *sqrt((xcoord-@XX)*(xcoord - @XX) +
      (ycoord - @yy)*(ycoord - @YY)))
from minisumdata);

/* RESULT OUTPUT */
```

```
select @XX as X_Coordinate, @YY as Y_Coordinate, @OBJ
       as Rectangular_Metric, @OBJ2 as Euclidean_Metric;
```

This particular query has both the standard Euclidean norm and the Manhattan norm used as output. The Euclidean norm serves as the shortest distance from potential sites to a facility while the Manhattan norm is equivalent to the distance cars would have to drive from one site to the optimal site. Both may be used by managers in making decisions to build facilities at particular locations.

8.3 Euler-Maruyama Method

The final stored procedure I am including in this text dabbles in a field of applied mathematics that is a personal favorite of mine, numerical analysis applied to stochastic differential equations. The first numerical scheme associated with this field is the Euler-Maruyama Method, or the Stochastic Euler Method. It is a method that gives an approximation to a Gaussian random process and is based on the Euler Method from differential equations. There are more advanced schemes also based on deterministic schemes, but this is one is usually the first one introduced.

```
Delimiter \\
create procedure EulerMaruyama(
in leftend float,
in rightend float,
in N int,
in initcon float
)
Begin

/*Setting up initial values for loop */

Set @h = (rightend - leftend)/N;
Set @t = leftend;
Set @w = initcon;
Set @i = 1;
create temporary table StochEulerTable( i float, approx float);
insert into StochEulerTable(i,approx)
values (@t, @w);

/* Drift = a(t,y) = -y + t + 1 is hard-coded into the loop.
Change this for other functions
Volatility = b(t,y) = y is hard-coded into the loop.
Change this for other functions.
Use Box-Mueller method for generating standard
 normal random variables*/
```

```
While @i <= N do
set @U1 = rand();
set @U2 = rand();
set @G1 = sqrt(-2*ln(@U1))*cos(2*Pi()*@U2);
set @G2 = sqrt(-2*ln(@U1))*sin(2*Pi()*@U2);
set @w = @w + @h * (-@w + @t + 1.0) + @w *(@G2 - @G1);
/* ^--- a(t,y) is here in ()  and b(t,y) is also here in
 second () with Noise*/
set @t = leftend + @i*@h;
set @i = @i+1;
insert into StochEulerTable(i,approx)
values (@t, @w);
 end while;
 end\\
Delimiter ;
```

As already mentioned, there are other schemes which are better suited for stochastic differential equations in the sense of convergence rates and stability. One of these schemes is the Milstein method. The Milstein method is provided below in a vector format, see if you can write this as a stored procedure.

$$Y_{n+1} = Y_n + Adt + b(W_{n+1} - W_n) + \frac{1}{2}b \cdot b'((W_{n+1} - W_n)^2 - dt)$$

where $A = a - 0.5(bb')$, a is the drift function and b is the volatility function. b' is the transpose of the volatility function (in one-dimension there is no change). W corresponds to a standard Gaussian random variable and dt is the time step. If you can get this working, see if you generalize this to a k-dimensional scheme. You have the tools, the knowledge and probably by now and most important, confidence in experiencing success. You *can* do this!

Chapter 9

Concluding Remarks

This text contains several stored procedures I believe would be helpful to students and faculty in an undergraduate mathematics course. You may be wondering why there is no linear algebra or other computations involving matrices. MySQL is a database language after all and things like the χ^2 tests for independence or matrix operations should be natural in MySQL. The reasons why these topics are not demonstrated here are, as most experts agree, that trying to perform these tasks requires too much coding, it dampens the performance of the code and MySQL is just not designed for these types of computations. It is not impossible to do, but this is not in keeping with the spirit of the text. This reference is designed to show the very basics of stored procedures applied to common tasks in many introductory mathematics courses.

The MySQL and SQL languages are common tools in corporate and industry. I can speak from experience that when I have MySQL and SQL experience on my resume, hiring managers eyes seem to light up a little more when compared to my putting *Mathematica* or *Maple* experience. This is due, in part, to the fact that many businesses use SQL or MySQL in their day-to-day operations and seems to be more expansive in its usefulness than these other software packages. Hopefully this text will help students gain a competitive advantage when applying for positions after their academics are complete. It is also my hope that instructors will take note of this powerful and beneficial tool in their classrooms and begin introducing it in courses that are computationally intensive, but perhaps not streamlined for career mathematicians or statisticians. I wish to thank you for taking the time to read over the text and I hope you have gained an interest to learn more about SQL and MySQL.

Chapter 10

Bibliography

1. Abramowitz, Milton and Irene A. Stegun. Handbook of Mathematical Functions. Dover Publications, New York, 1965.

2. Brophy, Alfred L. *Approximation of the Inverse Normal Distribution Function*. Behavior Research Methods, Instuments and Computers, 17(3), pg. 415 - 417, 1985.

3. Burden, Richard L. and J. Douglas Faires. *Numerical Analysis*. 4th ed. PWS-Kent Publishing Co. Boston, 1989. ISBN: 0-534-91585.

4. Fan, Lianghuo. *A Generalization of Synthetic Division and A General Theorem of Division of Polynomials*. Mathematical Medley Vol 30, No. 1 pp. 30-37, June 2003.

5. Hungerford, Thomas W. *Abstract Algebra: An Introduction* 2nd ed. Saunders College Publishing. 1997. ISBN: 0-03-010559-5.

6. Kloeden, Peter E., Eckhard Platen and Henri Shurz. *Numerical Solution of SDE Through Computer Experiments*. Springer, Berlin, 1997. ISBN: 3-430-57074-8.

7. Kloeden, Peter E. and Eckhard Platen. *Numerical Solution of Stochastic Differential Equations*. Springer, Berlin, 1995. ISBN: 3-540-54062-8.

8. Lial, Margaret L., Thomas W. Hungerford and Charles D. Miller. *Mathematics with Applications: Finite Version*. 6th ed. Harper Collins College Publishers, 1996. ISBN: 0-673-99274-8.

9. Thomas, Jr., George B., Maurice D. Weir, Joel Haas and Frank R. Giordano. *Thomas' Calculus: Early Transcendentals*. 11th ed., Pearson, Boston, 2008. ISBN: 0-321-49575-6.

10. Triola, Mario F. *Elementary Statistics Using Excel*. 4th ed. Addison-Wesley, Boston, 2010. ISBN: 0-321-56496-0.

www.ingramcontent.com/pod-product-compliance
Lightning Source LLC
Chambersburg PA
CBHW060203060326
40690CB00018B/4225